D1309597

The Reference Shelf®

U.S. Election System

Edited by Paul McCaffrey

Editorial Advisor Lynn M. Messina

The Reference Shelf
Volume 76 • Number 4

The H. W. Wilson Company
2004

The Reference Shelf

The books in this series contain reprints of articles, excerpts from books, addresses on current issues, and studies of social trends in the United States and other countries. There are six separately bound numbers in each volume, all of which are usually published in the same calendar year. Numbers one through five are each devoted to a single subject, providing background information and discussion from various points of view and concluding with a subject index and comprehensive bibliography that lists books, pamphlets, and abstracts of additional articles on the subject. The final number of each volume is a collection of recent speeches, and it contains a cumulative speaker index. Books in the series may be purchased individually or on subscription.

Library of Congress has cataloged this title as follows:

U.S. election system / edited by Paul McCaffrey.
     p. cm. — (The reference shelf; v. 76, no. 4)
     Includes bibliographical references and index.
     ISBN 0-8242-1036-0
     1. Elections—United States. 2. Voting—United States. 3. Political parties—United States. 4. Presidential candidates—United States. 5. Campaign funds—United States. 6. Presidents—United States—Election—2000. I. Title: US election system. II. McCaffrey, Paul, 1977–III. Series.

JK1976.U217 2004
324'.0973—dc22

                               2004053020

Cover: AP Photo/*The Oklahoman*, Paul B. Southerland

Visit H.W. Wilson's Web site: www.hwwilson.com

Printed in the United States of America

Contents

Preface

Since the ratification of the Constitution in 1788, every four years Americans have gone to the polls to elect a president. Though convulsed by civil war and domestic strife, economic depression and overseas conflict, the United States has never once deviated from this tradition; and more often than not, by virtue of America's long-dominant two-party system, voters have registered their preference for one of two major candidates. In the early days of the Republic, the choice was between Federalists and Democratic-Republicans, later Democrats and Whigs, and currently Democrats and Republicans. Other traditions have endured as well: The electoral college remains the legal framework of our elections, and money, in the form of campaign contributions, continues to influence the process.

Nevertheless, the sense of permanence and simplicity implied by these long-standing customs is not as clear-cut as it may seem. In the early days of the republic, only property-owning white males were allowed to vote. As our notions of equality and justice evolved, the franchise was gradually extended, until today nearly all American citizens over the age of 18, black or white, rich or poor, men or women, can voice their selections through the ballot box. While the Republicans and Democrats have maintained their preeminence for well over a century, the parties, their core beliefs, and their constituencies have undergone major alterations throughout their respective histories. In addition, the manner in which candidates are selected by the major parties has changed drastically over the years. Nominating conventions developed early in the 19th century, once important, decisive, and combative gatherings where party insiders used to muster up delegates to support one candidate or another, have since become staged coronations for candidates who have emerged in prior months in state-by-state primary elections among party members. Today, the Iowa caucus for Democrats and the Iowa straw poll for Republicans, followed by the New Hampshire primary and subsequent state contests, decide a party's nominee. Though money has always been a factor in election campaigns, with candidates buying advertisements in assorted mediums to communicate their messages to the people, its pernicious influence has become an issue among voters who feel that candidates have become the servants of their contributors and not their constituents. To address this problem, Congress passed the McCain-Feingold campaign finance reform bill, a significant renovation of the laws of political fund-raising.

This book's first section examines the essential framework and history of the United States' electoral system. It begins by exploring the evolution of voting rights in America, explaining when and how the franchise was expanded, and then offers cases for and against the electoral college. One highly potent outgrowth of the electoral college examined in this chapter is the inordinate impact—particularly in our current, politically polarized electorate—of swing states and swing voters on national elections. On a more technical level, the chapter also examines voting technology, including the machines and ballots currently in use.

The dynamics of the two-party system form the thematic framework for the second chapter. The histories of the Republican and Democratic parties are examined with an emphasis on their current makeup and positions on various social, political, and economic issues. This section also explores the effects that positions and ideas advanced by third-party candidates have had on the major parties and the extent to which they have influenced the debate. Though a third-party candidate has never captured the presidency, the third parties themselves have not been entirely ineffective.

The third section analyzes the various processes the parties have used over the years to select their presidential nominees, providing a history of the Iowa caucus and straw poll, as well as the New Hampshire primary and state primaries as a whole. The section also examines the inner workings of political conventions and how they have evolved.

The fourth chapter describes the influence of money on political campaigns and the impact of the McCain-Feingold finance reform bill on the process, as well as other recent innovations, such as the increased use of the Internet in reaching out to potential donors. In addition, arguments are proffered for and against a proposal by which political candidates would be allowed a certain amount of free airtime to broadcast their messages to voters via radio and television. Proponents believe free airtime would diminish the influence of money and fund-raising on the political process, while opponents offer a somewhat different take. The chapter also analyzes the think tank, another means by which money enters the political realm.

The 2004 national election may be one of the most important in U.S. history. Consequently, the final section in this book examines the current campaign, focusing on the races for president, between President George W. Bush and Senator John F. Kerry of Massachusetts; for the House of Representatives; and for the Senate. Selected articles highlight the dynamics of the race, including how the war in Iraq, the state of the economy, and other concerns may influence voters, while others consider groups expected to play a decisive role in the outcome, such as Hispanics and women, while others attempt to predict the winners by examining corollary issues that may impact the results, such as congressional redistricting and celebrity endorsements.

In conclusion, I would like to thank the many periodical publishers who have so generously granted permission to reprint their articles in these pages. I also must express my gratitude to the many associates at the H.W. Wilson Company who helped put this book together, especially Lynn Messina, Sandra Watson, and Jennifer Peloso. Thanks also to Gray Young, Norris Smith, Rich Stein, Mari Rich, and Clifford Thompson.

Paul McCaffrey
August 2004

I. The Basics: Voting and the Electoral College

Editor's Introduction

For most Americans, the concept of one person, one vote seems an eminently reasonable—indeed the *only* reasonable—foundation for a democratic government. Many would be surprised to learn that in United States elections universal suffrage is rather a recent phenomena, and that even today the majority does not always rule. These facts contribute to the two major paradoxes of the U.S. democratic system. First, voting rights—popular rhetoric aside—have never been as egalitarian as our ideals would suggest; initially only the provenance of property-owning white males, the franchise was gradually extended over the years to include all races and genders, but this process was not easy or quick. The second paradox is the electoral college, the constitutionally mandated process through which we elect our presidents; ostensibly democratic in nature, the electoral college has at times nullified majority rule and thus served antidemocratic purposes.

The first article in this chapter, by Elizabeth M. Yang from the *Update on Law-Related Education*, addresses the first paradox, charting the historical evolution of voting rights in America and the moments over the centuries when previously disenfranchised groups were finally granted their democratic voice. It is interesting to note, however, that the right to vote is not explicitly guaranteed in the Constitution.

The second paradox—the at-times antidemocratic nature of the electoral college—was vividly illustrated in the 2000 election when Vice President Al Gore received half a million more votes nationally than the eventual winner, Governor George W. Bush. Gore's singular defeat was a function of the electoral college, which has been in use since 1788. To become president, the Constitution states, a candidate does not need to win the popular vote, but rather must capture a majority in the electoral college.

In the 2000 election, following Bush's controversial triumph in Florida which, once awarded, gave him the necessary electoral votes to claim the presidency, many debated the efficacy of the electoral college. In this chapter, Democratic Senator Byron Dorgan of North Dakota argues in *Roll Call* that the system works well by ensuring that minorities, small states, and rural voters have an impact on national elections, while Jamin B. Raskin, for *American Prospect*, maintains that the electoral college sabotages democracy and is an ongoing embarrassment that has long outlived its usefulness.

One of the outgrowths of the electoral college is the increased importance of certain "swing" states. These states tend to be closely divided along partisan lines and so can tilt either way in a particular election; sometimes, as was the case with Florida in 2000, these states can determine the outcome of a national election. In a piece for *Atlantic Monthly*, Joshua Green examines the huge impact of the so-called swing voter in swing states.

On a different level, the Florida debacle in 2000 illustrated another shortcoming of American elections: Voting technology—the machines and ballots themselves—has not been up to the task. In Florida poorly constructed or confusing ballots caused votes to be discounted, effectively disenfranchising voters and calling into question the integrity of the whole election. Afterwards, many believed that improved technology—touch-screen electronic voting, for example—could cure the system of its ills. Two pieces in this chapter, one by Mary Wiltenburg for the *Christian Science Monitor* and one by Jonathan Krim for the *Washington Post*, offer differing arguments on whether technology might prevent a redux of the 2000 vote-counting controversy.

History of Voting in the United States[1]

By Elizabeth M. Yang
Update on Law-Related Education, Fall 1996

Voting is an integral part of American citizenship. It is a fundamental right and privilege of democracy that quite often is neither appreciated nor understood. Over 200 years ago, only a limited part of the population was allowed to cast a ballot, and now nearly all citizens over the age of 18 are entitled to vote.

Black's Law Dictionary defines the word *vote* as "suffrage or the expression of one's will, preference, or choice." The ability to express an opinion through voting is a concept that is easily understood and has become a part of daily life. After all, some form of voting can be found at all levels of society—in politics, schools, social situations, and the workplace. Suffrage, on the other hand, is a concept that is not as easily grasped or perceived. A further look into *Black's Law Dictionary* reveals that *suffrage* is defined as "a vote; the act of voting; the right or privilege of casting a vote at public elections." This definition is often ignored by or unknown to the average citizen. In order to fully understand suffrage, or rather the concept of voting as a privilege in our society, we must examine the relevant amendments to the Constitution and the accompanying landmarks in the history of the United States, which have resulted in the current electoral process.

The Right to Vote

Many people would be amazed to know that the Constitution originally allowed the states to bestow the right to vote only on white males who either owned property or paid poll taxes. Article I, Section 2 refers to "the People of the several States" having the right to vote for members of the House of Representatives, which at that time meant adult white males. Approximately 6 percent of the adult male population was actually eligible to vote because individual states were able to dictate various religious and property requirements. By 1850, all states had abolished these, and thus the number of adult white males who were entitled to vote grew, but the poll tax still remained a barrier to some. The fact that all adult white males were still not eligible to vote even 50 years after the formation of the United States illustrates the long process that the nation would have to undergo in order to expand the voting franchise even further. Amendments to the Constitution have provided the basis for extending the right to vote to other parts of the population.

Fifteenth Amendment—The Elimination of Racial Barriers to Voting

The aftermath of the Civil War created another opening for the expansion of the right to vote. The groundwork was laid in 1865, when the Thirteenth Amendment to the Constitution out-lawed slavery, and in 1868, the Fourteenth Amendment granted citizenship to all people born or naturalized in the United States. Finally, in 1870, the Fifteenth Amendment was adopted, which stated, "The right of citizens of the United States to vote shall not be denied or abridged by the United States or by any State on account of race, color, or previous condition of servitude."

By 1870, as a matter of federal law, the right to vote had been extended to all male citizens of the United States. The reality of the matter was, of course, rather far from fact. In the South, various methods, such as poll taxes, grandfather clauses, and literacy tests, were used to deny African-American males the ability to exercise their right to vote. Poll taxes created a monetary barrier to voting that excluded even poor white males. Several Southern states adopted grandfather clauses that excepted anyone who had voted before 1866—or who was a descendant of someone who had voted before that time—from being subject to other restrictions to voting, such as literacy tests, educational or "good character" tests, or poll taxes. Literacy tests were administered in a discriminatory fashion, ranging from requiring the basic ability to read and write to requiring the ability to read and understand the U.S. or state constitution. In other words, African Americans were faced with barriers that white males were exempt from, by virtue of the fact that white males or their ancestors had voted in a period when African Americans could not vote.

Nineteenth Amendment—Women's Right to Vote

In 1920, the Constitution was again amended, this time to declare that "the right of citizens of the United States to vote shall not be denied or abridged by the United States or by any state on account of sex." This amendment was the result of the women's suffrage movement, which originated in the late 1800s and early 1900s. Women now worked both inside and outside the home and were becoming a growing and united voice in the quest for the vote. Women across the country began to demonstrate, picket, and make speeches in support of their right to vote. In 1872, Susan B. Anthony voted in a national election and was subsequently convicted of voting without having a legal basis to do so. Critics of extending the vote portrayed women as being weak and lacking both the ability and the temperament necessary to make the decision involved in casting a ballot. In the West, where women, of necessity, were more active as laborers and wage earners, the women's suffrage movement was more successful. By 1912, nine of the eleven Western states had granted women the full right to vote in state and local elections.

The onset of World War I in 1914 provided the final push for the suffrage movement. Women began to protest even more vehemently that it was absurd for the United States to deny female citizens the right to vote when the country was in the midst of fighting a war based on world democracy. On August 18, 1920, Tennessee became the 36th state to approve the Nineteenth Amendment, which was ratified on August 26, 1920. Women were at last given the vote, 137 years after white men.

Twenty-third Amendment

When the District of Columbia was founded in 1802, from portions of Virginia and Maryland, the residents were denied the right to vote in presidential elections. In 1960, with the adoption of the Twenty-third Amendment to the Constitution, the residents of the District were given the right to vote.

Twenty-fourth Amendment—The End of the Poll Tax

In 1964, the poll tax was abolished. Although the majority of the states had already rescinded their laws instituting taxes as a barrier to voting, five Southern states continued to require citizens to pay to vote. The Twenty-fourth Amendment effectively denied the states the ability to consider a citizen's economic status as a factor in the voting process.

Voting Rights Act of 1965

The repeal of poll taxes should have opened the polls to all citizens, yet a disproportionate number of African Americans in the South had still not registered to vote. The Voting Rights Act of 1965 was passed by Congress in an effort to increase voter registration by repealing the requirements for literacy tests and similar devices, which denied otherwise eligible citizens the right to vote. The statute affected only states that had registered less than 50 percent of the voting-age population by November 1, 1964.

In 1970, Congress passed legislation prohibiting uses of literacy tests and requiring that bilingual ballots be used in areas where at least 5 percent of the population could not speak or understand English. The Voting Rights Act resulted in massive voter registration drives by African Americans and other minorities, thus effectively broadening the right to vote.

Twenty-sixth Amendment—Reduction of the Voting Age

In 1971, Congress passed a bill that, when approved by the states as the Twenty-sixth Amendment, extended voting rights to those citizens 18 (from 21) years and older. The driving force behind this extension of voting rights was the student protest movement that sprang up in opposition to the Vietnam War. Just as women in the early 20th century had used the First World War to argue for their right to vote, students began to decry the fact that they were considered old enough to fight for their country, but not old enough to vote.

Conclusion

The extensions of the right to vote to all United States citizens 18 or older, regardless of race or gender—with the exception of convicted felons and the mentally incompetent—did not come about without great struggle and determination. It is interesting to note how the events of American history helped provide each part of the population with the right to vote. The Revolutionary War gave the vote; the Civil War enabled African Americans to be recognized as citizens and thus enabled them to vote; the First World War became the focal point for women's right to vote; and the Vietnam War reduced the age for voting. The passion that resulted from those earlier trying times should not be forgotten or forsaken.

The exercise of one's right to vote is, unfortunately, not as common as one would think. People in many countries struggle daily for the opportunity to voice their opinions freely and without fear of reprisal. Suffrage is, indeed, a privilege and a right that should not be taken lightly or for granted. Voting is not only an expression of opinion, but a fundamental and inherent part of citizenship—as it allows individuals to let their voices be heard.

Amendments to the Constitution: Voting

Amendment XV—Race is no bar to voting. Ratified February 3, 1870.

1. The right of citizens of the United States to vote shall not be denied or abridged by the United States or by any State on account of race, color, or previous condition of servitude.
2. The Congress shall have power to enforce this article by appropriate legislation.

Amendment XIX—Women's suffrage. Ratified August 18, 1920.
The right of citizens of the United States to vote shall not be denied or abridged by the United States or by any State on account of sex.
Congress shall have power to enforce this article by appropriate legislation.

Amendment XXIII—Presidential vote for District of Columbia. Ratified March 29, 1961.

1. The District constituting the seat of Government of the United States shall appoint in such manner as the Congress may direct: A number of electors of President and Vice President equal to the whole number of Senators and Representatives in Congress to which the District would be entitled if it were a State, but in no event more than the least populous State; they shall be in addition to those appointed by the States, but they shall be considered, for the purposes of the election of President and Vice President, to be electors appointed by a State; and they shall meet in the District and perform such duties as provided by the twelfth article of amendment.
2. The Congress shall have power to enforce this article by appropriate legislation.

Amendment XXIV—Poll tax barred. Ratified January 23, 1964.

1. The right of citizens of the United States to vote in any primary or other election for President or Vice President, for electors for President or Vice President, or for Senator or Representative in Congress, shall not be denied or abridged by the United States or any State by reason of failure to pay any poll tax or other tax.
2. The Congress shall have power to enforce this article by appropriate legislation.

Amendment XXVI—Voting age set to 18 years. Ratified July 1, 1971.

1. The right of citizens of the United States, who are eighteen years of age or older, to vote shall not be denied or abridged by the United States or by any State on account of age.
2. The Congress shall have power to enforce this article by appropriate legislation.

Electoral College Works Quietly, Just As Founders Intended[2]

BY SEN. BYRON DORGAN
ROLL CALL, JANUARY 15, 2001

In the wake of the 2000 election, the Electoral College has taken a few hits. We hear that it is a rusty relic from a bygone era, and that time has passed it by.

This is unfortunate. The Electoral College works, quietly and in ways we are inclined to take for granted. To abolish it would not solve any pressing problem, but it would create some new ones.

The genius of the Constitution lies in its inspired practicality. It was not the work of philosophers gathered to construct an ideal hypothetical republic. The Constitutional Convention consisted of seasoned men of affairs.

They represented different regions, states, and interests. They had been through the travails of the American Revolution and the Articles of Confederation.

They were not without blind spots or faults, but they had a grip on the crucial question. What institutional arrangements might enable electoral democracy to work on a scale and over a geographical expanse never tried before in history nor even contemplated?

In an atmosphere of large tensions and conflicts, the delegates wrestled with concrete difficulties, not just abstract propositions, and the result was an ingenious plan.

The elected government would consist of three parts. There would be a House of Representatives elected by popular vote, a Senate in which each state would have an equal voice regardless of size, and a president elected through a sort of extension of the two. The voters of each state get a say in choosing the president in proportion to their states' representation in Congress.

Thus was born the Electoral College. If we somehow could tell the Founders that this arrangement was not ideal, they would agree. In fact, they would probably take it as a compliment. After all, their goal was a system that could work, and in that they succeeded. No arrangement for constitutional democracy has lasted so long on so large a scale. We should pause before casting the Founders' work aside.

The Electoral College makes an inviting target. It is as quirky as the corridors of the Capitol. Yet the eccentricity of the system is what makes it work.

---

2. Article by Sen. Byron Dorgan from *Roll Call* January 15, 2001. Copyright © *Roll Call*. Reprinted with permission.

Born in compromise, the system accommodates the tensions that otherwise could cause chronic conflict. It gives voice to regional concerns, such as farming and water issues, and it amplifies the impact of minorities on the big stage of presidential politics. The nation is the better for it.

As a Senator from a rural state, I'm naturally concerned about all of this. Presidential candidates pay little enough attention to states like mine. Take away the Electoral College and candidates might bypass us completely. Why travel to Grand Forks when you can spend the time trolling for votes in Los Angeles or New York with a much greater payoff per hour spent?

This boost for smaller states was part of the original agreement that brought our country together. It is warp and woof of our federal system. But small states and rural areas are not the only ones who benefit. Minorities of all kinds gain as well.

Under the Electoral College system, African-Americans, for example, carry more weight because they are significant blocs in electorally vital states. States such as New York, North Carolina and, yes, even Florida can swing one way or the other depending on this vote.

Under the Electoral College system, African-Americans . . . carry more weight because they are significant blocs in electorally vital states.

So politicians must pay heed, and the same goes for Hispanics, Asian-Americans, and many others. Asian-Americans are numerically significant in the politics of California. They are less so in the national populace. A strict popular vote for president would dilute their influence, and that would not be good for Asian-Americans or for the country.

This is not to say the Electoral College system is beyond improvement. For one thing, electors should be bound to honor the choice of the voters.

If the voters choose George W. Bush, then the electors from that state should have to vote for him. There should be no speculation about electors changing sides, as there was during the last election. Historically, such "faithless electors" have been rare, but they should never exist, period.

Second, more states should adjust their voting systems in a way that provides more individual choice and more voice to minority concerns. For example, both Maine and Nebraska now allocate their electoral votes according to the winners in each Congressional district. If Vice President Al Gore had won in a particular district, then he would have received the electoral votes from that district, even if he didn't win statewide. Such a system forces candidates to broaden their appeals—and makes each vote potentially more important.

The current attack on the Electoral College is off-point to begin with. The Electoral College was not the reason for the ballot problems in Florida in November. It did not cause the purging of the voter rolls, nor did it cause a single hanging chad. Abolish the Electoral College and every antiquated voting machine in this country will remain exactly where it is.

We need to upgrade this nation's voting system, and we can. That doesn't mean scrapping the Electoral College, though. Minorities and rural areas should have a voice in our presidential politics, and the Electoral College helps ensure that they do.

If the system "be not perfect, it is at least excellent," as Alexander Hamilton put it. That's not so bad, as we might say today.

Amendments to the Constitution: Electoral College

Article. II.

Section. 1.

Clause 1: The executive Power shall be vested in a President of the United States of America. He shall hold his Office during the Term of four Years, and, together with the Vice President, chosen for the same Term, be elected, as follows:

Clause 2: Each State shall appoint, in such Manner as the Legislature thereof may direct, a Number of Electors, equal to the whole Number of Senators and Representatives to which the State may be entitled in the Congress: but no Senator or Representative, or Person holding an Office of Trust or Profit under the United States, shall be appointed an Elector.

Clause 3: The Electors shall meet in their respective States, and vote by Ballot for two Persons, of whom one at least shall not be an Inhabitant of the same State with themselves. And they shall make a List of all the Persons voted for, and of the Number of Votes for each; which List they shall sign and certify, and transmit sealed to the Seat of the Government of the United States, directed to the President of the Senate. The President of the Senate shall, in the Presence of the Senate and House of Representatives, open all the Certificates, and the Votes shall then be counted. The Person having the greatest Number of Votes shall be the President, if such Number be a Majority of the whole Number of Electors appointed; and if there be more than one who have such Majority, and have an equal Number of Votes, then the House of Representatives shall immediately chuse by Ballot one of them for President; and if no Person have a Majority, then from the five highest on the List the said House shall in like Manner chuse the President. But in chusing the President, the Votes shall be taken by States, the Representation from each State having one Vote; A quorum for this Purpose shall consist of a Member or Members from two thirds of the States, and a Majority of all the States shall be necessary to a Choice. In every Case, after the Choice of the President, the Person having the greatest Number of Votes of the Electors shall be the Vice President. But if there should remain two or more who have equal Votes, the Senate shall chuse from them by Ballot the Vice President.

Clause 4: The Congress may determine the Time of chusing the Electors, and the Day on which they shall give their Votes; which Day shall be the same throughout the United States.

Amendment XII—Choosing the President, Vice-President. Ratified June 15, 1804.

The Electors shall meet in their respective states, and vote by ballot for President and Vice-President, one of whom, at least, shall not be an inhabitant of the same state with themselves; they shall name in their ballots the person voted for as President, and in distinct ballots the person voted for as Vice-President, and they shall make distinct lists of all persons voted for as President, and of all persons voted for as Vice-President and of the number of votes for each, which lists they shall sign and certify, and transmit sealed to the seat of the government of the United States, directed to the President of the Senate;

The President of the Senate shall, in the presence of the Senate and House of Representatives, open all the certificates and the votes shall then be counted;

The person having the greatest Number of votes for President, shall be the President, if such number be a majority of the whole number of Electors appointed; and if no person have such majority, then from the persons having the highest numbers not exceeding three on the list of those voted for as President, the House of Representatives shall choose immediately, by ballot, the President. But in choosing the President, the votes shall be taken by states, the representation from each state having one vote; a quorum for this purpose shall consist of a member or members from two-thirds of the states, and a majority of all the states shall be necessary to a choice. And if the House of Representatives shall not choose a President whenever the right of choice shall devolve upon them, before the fourth day of March next following, then the Vice-President shall act as President, as in the case of the death or other constitutional disability of the President.

The person having the greatest number of votes as Vice-President, shall be the Vice-President, if such number be a majority of the whole number of Electors appointed, and if no person have a majority, then from the two highest numbers on the list, the Senate shall choose the Vice-President; a quorum for the purpose shall consist of two-thirds of the whole number of Senators, and a majority of the whole number shall be necessary to a choice. But no person constitutionally ineligible to the office of President shall be eligible to that of Vice-President of the United States.

A Right to Vote[3]

BY JAMIN B. RASKIN
THE AMERICAN PROSPECT, AUGUST 27, 2001

Of everything we learned about American politics from the Supreme Court's ruling in *Bush v. Gore* last December, nothing was more important than the Court's insistence that the people still have "no federal constitutional right to vote." We (the people) have only the voting privileges our states choose to grant us. If the Florida legislature wishes to select presidential electors without public input, the people shall not stand in the way.

More than presidential elections are at stake here. Several weeks before *Bush v. Gore,* for example, the Supreme Court upheld a 2–1 federal-district-court decision that rejected an equal-protection attack on the denial of voting rights and congressional representation to the more than half a million U.S. citizens who live in the District of Columbia. "The Equal Protection Clause does not protect the right of all citizens to vote," the lower-court ruling stated, "but rather the right 'of all *qualified* citizens to vote.'" Thus two Clinton-appointed federal judges overruled the senior judge on the panel—Louis Oberdorfer, a Jimmy Carter appointee—and found that however "inequitable" the condition of D.C.'s residents may be, simply being subject to federal taxation and military conscription does not confer on Washingtonians a right to vote and to be represented in the Senate and the House or other governing institutions.

This may be a conservative reading of the Constitution, but it is black-letter law. True, the Constitution contains specific, hard-won language in the 15th and 19th Amendments that forbids discrimination in voting on the basis of race or sex. But these prohibitions don't establish a universal right to vote. Thus, Congress cannot selectively disenfranchise women in the District of Columbia but can, and does, render all of its residents voiceless in Congress by denying them representation in the House and Senate. The Florida legislature may not (theoretically, anyway) dismiss only the votes of African Americans; but as the Supreme Court kindly reminded us in *Bush v. Gore,* it can dismiss everyone's votes. Likewise, Florida cannot selectively deny African-American ex-convicts the right to vote in state and federal elections, but it disenfranchises all ex-offenders—some 400,000 of them.

---

3. Reprinted with permission from *The American Prospect*, Volume 12, Number 15: August 27, 2001. The American Prospect, 11 Beacon Street, Suite 1120, Boston, MA 02108. All rights reserved.

The nation's tolerance for disenfranchisement in the 21st century is quite exceptional. The constitutions of at least 135 nations—including our fellow North American countries, Canada and Mexico—explicitly guarantee citizens the right to vote and to be represented at all levels of government. In fact, every new constitution adopted over the past decade makes the right to vote the very foundation of government.

Constitutional silence on a basic right to vote leaves the United States in miserable, backward company. By my count, only Azerbaijan, Chechnya, Indonesia, Iran, Iraq, Jordan, Libya, Pakistan, Singapore, and, of course, the United Kingdom (whose phony doctrine of "virtual representation" the colonists rebelled against centuries ago) still leave voting rights out of their constitutions and therefore to the whims of state officials. This sin of omission violates—to the extent that anyone cares—the International Covenant on Civil and Political Rights and numerous other international conventions inspired by the democratic triumph over totalitarianism in World War II.

> *Constitutional silence on a basic right to vote leaves the United States in miserable, backward company.*

It is time for American progressives to engage in serious constitutional politics on behalf of the right to vote. This is the only way to redeem the chaos of the 2000 presidential election and to begin to ensure that such an assault on democracy will never be repeated. Consider this proposal for a 28th Amendment:

SECTION 1. Citizens of the United States have the right to vote in primary and general elections for President and Vice President, for electors for President and Vice President, for Representatives and Senators in the Congress, and for executive and legislative officers of their state, district, and local legislatures, and such right shall not be denied or abridged by the United States or any State.

SECTION 2. The right of citizens of the United States to vote and to participate in elections on an equal basis shall not be denied or abridged by the United States or any State on account of political-party affiliation or prior condition of incarceration.

SECTION 3. The District constituting the seat of Government of the United States shall elect Senators and Representatives in the Congress in such number and such manner as it would be entitled if it were a State.

SECTION 4. The Congress shall have power to enforce this article by appropriate legislation.

A campaign for such an amendment would give coherence and energy to the scattered efforts across the country to reform the anachronistic, malleable electoral structures that exist in literally thousands of self-regulated jurisdictions. The movement behind the amendment would help sweep away not only disenfranchisement but reactionary partisan and sectional opposition to a number of democratic reforms: the push to upgrade and equalize voting technology and machinery, the effort to require equal and adequate funding of voting systems, and unsung efforts by third parties and independents to end discriminatory practices against candidates and voters based on party identification. (In many states, "major party" candidates automatically appear on the ballot while "minor party" candidates must collect tens of thousands of signatures to secure the right to compete. Along similar lines, the Supreme Court in 1998 upheld the partisan gerrymandering of government-run candidate debates.)

Instead of treating these seemingly disparate causes as a patchwork of local grievances, a right-to-vote amendment would elevate the agenda of electoral reform to a matter of national self-definition and fundamental constitutional values. The reason that the *Bush v. Gore* decision—that unthinkably radical statement about the urgent need for absolute equality of voting procedures and standards across county lines—won't work in these other cases can be found in the disclaimer appended by the Supreme Court's conservative majority: "Our consideration is limited to the present circumstances, for the problem of equal protection in election processes generally presents many complexities." Like Cinderella's dress, the conservatives' gallant defense of voting rights after last year's presidential election turned to rags at midnight.

In Yale Law School Professor Bruce Ackerman's phrase, "constitutional moments" don't come around all that often, so it is crucial to seize the political opportunity created by the continuing scandal of the 2000 election. But even when the time is right for change, reformers face hard choices.

In this case, the biggest headache is the electoral college. A deliberately undemocratic institution that made the popular-vote loser (George W. Bush, by more than half a million votes) the president of the United States, the electoral college is an international embarrassment. Since the nation's founding, it has entrenched the power of the slave states (four of the first five presidents were slave masters), white supremacy (throughout the 20th century, southern states ran regional candidates and manipulated the electoral college to thwart the civil rights movement), and now the Republican electoral-college coalition, which represents a minority of voters nationally and a much smaller minority of the people. George W. Bush took every single electoral-college vote in the South and found a majority of his electoral-college votes there. Meanwhile, the majority of African Americans, more than 20 million, live in the South and gave Al Gore better than 90 percent of their vote. Yet because of the winner-take-all method of distributing electoral-college votes, black votes in the South—even when counted—had zero impact on the election.

In a more rational world, abolition of the electoral college would be a key part of a 28th Amendment. But too many states and senators buy in to the myth that the electoral college helps them. It is extremely unlikely that even a simple majority of states would ratify an amendment abolishing the electoral college, much less the 38 required constitutionally. Only a handful of senators, including New York Democrat Hillary Clinton, have voiced support for the idea; and the Senate, where small states hold great power, will be a long time coming around on the issue. As outrageous as the situation is, it does not make sense to load down a right-to-vote amendment with this kind of baggage. Few things would stop this amendment, but the electoral college is one of them. That issue's time will come.

Some may wonder about the wisdom of tackling the disenfranchisement of Washingtonians and ex-convicts. But these battles of basic principle are eminently winnable. Public-opinion polls show that commanding majorities of the people favor giving residents of Washington, D.C., equal voting rights in Congress, and the rallying cry of "No taxation without representation" has persistent and broad cross-partisan appeal.

The amendment would not restore rights to incarcerated citizens—only to those who have already served their time and been released. Disenfranchisement of 1.4 million citizens, disproportionate numbers of whom are people of color, makes no sense. It drives ex-offenders away from political participation and civic belonging precisely at the moment they need to be encouraged and invited back into mainstream society. Most states already extend voting rights to this group and have crime rates no higher than the 13 states that turn a period of former incarceration into a permanent civic disability. Americans are fair-minded people and most would be shocked to learn that one in three African-American men has permanently lost the vote in Florida because of a prior felony conviction. A provision protecting former inmates' voting rights would have a good chance to make it through Congress and be adopted by the states.

It now falls to the people to bring the U.S. Constitution into line with the fundamental tenets of American political thought that emerged in the aftermath of the modern civil rights movement. As Robert P. Moses and Charles Cobb tell us in their important new book *Radical Equations,* the concept of "one person, one vote" in the early 1960s gave "Mississippi sharecroppers and their allies" a principle of "common conceptual cohesion" that was taken up by the Justice Department and then embraced by the Warren Court in the redistricting cases. As Justice Hugo Black put it in 1964, "Our Constitution leaves no room for classification of people in a way that unnecessarily abridges [the right to vote]."

But universal suffrage, a radical axiom established by the blood and sweat of civil rights activists in the South, has steadily eroded on the conservative Rehnquist Court's watch. Over the past decade, the Supreme Court has dismantled congressional districts composed mostly of African Americans or Hispanics—districts brought into being by the Voting Rights Act of 1965—and in the course of doing so has inscribed into law a presumption that whites shall be in the majority. It has allowed states to deny voters the right to "write in" the candidates of their choice. And it has upheld state laws that ban "fusion" and thus deny new political parties the capacity to build by "cross-nominating" candidates and creating multiparty political coalitions.

The principles of universal suffrage and democracy now lie in tatters. Yet the American movement for "one person, one vote" has traveled around the world, from Poland to South Africa. The United States must now

> *The American movement for "one person, one vote" has traveled around the world.*

catch up with its own legacy. We must disprove the French observation, much deployed after the 2000 election, that the Americans have no antiques—except, of course, for the Constitution.

The political question is whether progressives, accustomed to fighting off countless proposed amendments by the right on issues like school prayer and flag desecration, can overcome their knee-jerk suspicion of all constitutional changes. Many liberals treat the Constitution like an untouchable religious text and the republic's founders as omniscient. This is ironic, for we have traditionally understood that the original Constitution was deeply compromised by white supremacy and fear of popular democracy. Many of the amendments enacted since the founding are suffrage amendments championed by progressives—most recently, the 23d Amendment (adopted in 1961), which gave residents of Washington, D.C., votes in the presidential electoral college; the 24th Amendment (1964), which banned poll taxes; and the 26th Amendment (1971), which extended the vote to 18-year-olds. Meaningful democratic politics requires an aggressive constitutional politics. Let them come at us with proposals about the flag, school prayer, and the Ten Commandments. We can return fire with the constitutional right to vote, which in a democracy must take moral precedence and logical priority over everything else.

Under Article V of the Constitution, an amendment requires either a two-thirds vote in both houses of Congress followed by ratification by three-fourths of the states or passage in a constitutional convention called upon the application of the legislatures of two-thirds of the states followed by ratification by three-fourths of the states. Starting with the League of Women Voters, the secretaries of state, the NAACP, journals of opinion, the labor movement, political parties that are willing to place democratic principle above factional designs, and the state legislatures, we should reach out to our fellow citizens and take the irresistible case for a voting-rights amendment to the people. Certain progressive members of Congress already see the logic of such an effort. Democratic Congressman Jesse Jackson, Jr., of Illinois has been arguing eloquently for a whole series of new constitutional rights, including health care and housing. His broader agenda is more complicated, but his spirit is perfect for the new century: We have to stop treating the Constitution like a fragile heirloom hidden away in the attic. And we must begin by providing what was missing when the Constitution was first drafted—the right of the people to vote and, therefore, to govern.

In Search of the Elusive Swing Voter[4]

By Joshua Green
Atlantic Monthly, January/February 2004

During the primary season we are accustomed to focusing on the drama and intrigue in a few important states such as New Hampshire and Iowa. A candidate who can win these, it is believed, is all but certain to carry the nomination. Suddenly that's less true than in years past. Because so many candidates are running, and because the contests are not winner-take-all, formerly inconsequential states such as Oklahoma, New Mexico, and even Delaware could be critical in determining who finally emerges as the next Democratic nominee. In contrast, we tend to view the general election as wide open, when in fact fewer and fewer states have determined the outcome in recent presidential elections. The reason for this is the growing polarization of the American electorate.

In fact, there is empirical evidence to suggest that this year's contest may be the most partisan in history. In the 2000 election less than 10 percent of Democrats voted for George W. Bush, and a similarly small percentage of Republicans voted for Al Gore—the lowest voter crossover ever documented. The Supreme Court's decision in *Bush v. Gore*, the Bush Administration's hard-nosed tactics, and the war in Iraq have only widened this divide.

As the American electorate becomes ever more polarized, the number of undecided voters and the number of states in which the two parties will truly compete have diminished considerably. Two decades ago as much as a third of the electorate was deemed to be in play, and there were grand debates, particularly in the Democratic Party, about whether the best way to win "swing" voters was to pursue a southern strategy or to target the Rocky Mountains. "A basic postulate of American politics today," says the political demographer Mark Gersh, a Democratic strategist, "is that the swing vote is much, much smaller than it used to be." Strategists in both parties have narrowed their focus to no more than 10 percent of the electorate (some have narrowed it even further), and both parties plan to seriously contest only about 15 states in November. This shrunken playing field, along with hardening lines in the electorate, all but guarantees a close race. That in turn limits the strategic possibili-

---

ties for both parties to the point where it is possible to predict in considerable detail what the next campaign will look like—even without knowing the identity of the Democratic nominee.

There is a widespread misperception that the course of a presidential campaign flows directly from the candidate's persona. Naturally, a Howard Dean campaign would differ in style and atmospherics from one featuring Wesley Clark or John Kerry or Richard Gephardt. But with so little room to maneuver, the Democratic formula for victory will depend less than ever on the identity of the nominee. Instead it will be dictated by geographic and demographic necessity—how best to cobble together the necessary 270 electoral votes. The candidate must carry a sufficient number of swing states, and success in each one will depend on highly specific combinations of constituencies and issues—many of which can already be identified. In other words, just as the genetic blueprint for human beings and chimpanzees is 95 percent identical, the campaign blueprint for the Democratic candidates will be nearly the same, regardless of which becomes the party's nominee.

The unprecedented closeness of the 2000 presidential election has had dramatic effects on the political world.

The unprecedented closeness of the 2000 presidential election has had dramatic effects on the political world, from the news media's hesitancy to call election results to the parties' renewed emphasis on voter turnout to the newfound superstition among speechwriters that they must prepare three versions of a candidate's election-night remarks: the dignified victory speech, the gracious concession, and a third in case the election is too close to call. To political demographers, who digest ungodly amounts of data in an effort to understand and predict the behavior of the American electorate, the 2000 contest provided a sort of Rosetta stone: a demographic snapshot of a nation in perfect balance, which has become the starting point for strategy in 2004.

All told, 12 states in the previous presidential election were decided by fewer than five percentage points. Along with two or three other states where demographic changes portend a similar closeness, they make up the battleground this year. The most significant states are scattered across the Pacific Northwest (Oregon, Washington), the Southwest (Arizona, Nevada, New Mexico), and the Rust Belt (Ohio, Pennsylvania, West Virginia), with outliers on the East Coast (Florida and New Hampshire) and others along a lengthy stretch of the Mississippi River, from Minnesota and Wisconsin down to Arkansas and Missouri. The next Democratic campaign will closely follow this map.

The Northwest. In numerical terms the most striking aspect of the 2000 election remains the number of votes Al Gore lost to Ralph Nader. "Democrats created an opening for Nader in 2000 by not taking the Green Party seriously enough until it was too late," says Doug Sosnik, a White House political director under Bill Clinton. To head off a similar catastrophe the Democratic nominee will probably begin his campaign with an early pilgrimage to the Pacific Northwest, where Green Party support is strongest, to quell a potential challenge. Such a move would not only strengthen the candidate's standing in Oregon and Washington, two states Gore won narrowly, but also provide a platform for talking about the environment—one of the few "wedge issues" available to Democrats, and an issue pollsters believe is the primary motivator for six percent of voters.

The South. The other great political truth revealed in 2000—and reinforced in 2002—is the Republicans' consolidation of the South. The long-standing axiom that the Democrats must carry southern states to win the presidency still holds sway among many political consultants, and at least partially accounts for the premium placed on southern candidates such as Wesley Clark and John Edwards. But Democratic strategists are increasingly aware that that goal has become nearly unattainable. With the exception of Florida, the South has trended away from the party. Bill Clinton's success in the 1990s was not indicative of a southern Democratic resurgence—rather, it masked this erosion. Georgia, which Clinton carried in 1992, went Republican in 1996. Arkansas, Kentucky, Louisiana, and Tennessee, which Clinton carried in both his elections, all followed suit in 2000. Thomas F. Schaller, a professor of political science at the University of Maryland, Baltimore County, warns, "Pursuing a southern strategy in 2004, instead of looking ahead to other areas, could relegate the party to minority status for years to come." Indeed, the futility of a southern strategy is tacitly acknowledged in the list of swing states that Democratic groups are planning to contest this year. Of the 17 states targeted by America Coming Together, a coalition of liberal interest groups aimed at mobilizing Democratic voters, only Florida and Arkansas are in the South.

> *[The] great political truth revealed in 2000 . . . is the Republicans' consolidation of the South.*

The Southwest. The Democrats' new area of opportunity is a swath of formerly Republican territory where an influx of Latinos and transplanted white Democrats is changing the demographic profile. Gore's lone win in this region was New Mexico, where his margin of victory was even narrower than his margin of defeat in Florida. But newly elected Democratic governors in Arizona and New Mexico and booming Hispanic populations there (25 percent and 42 percent, respectively) should persuade this year's nominee to spend considerable time and effort in the region. Nevada, too, has become a case study for Democratic optimism: although Bush carried the state in 2000, the Latino population surged by 15 percent in just the next two years; Clark County, which leans Democratic, is among the nation's fastest-growing counties; and Las Vegas, in that county, is rapidly unionizing. Furthermore, Nevada presents an enticing opportunity to raise the issue of Yucca Mountain, where President Bush recently decided to dump nuclear waste after vowing during his campaign not to do so.

Florida. Latinos, who have historically been identified with the Democratic Party, now represent an important swing vote. As it became clear in the closing weeks of the 2000 campaign that several battleground states would go down to the wire, the Republicans spent an unprecedented amount of money on Spanish-language television advertising; overall, they ended up spending more than twice as much as the Democrats. According to Adam J. Segal, the director of the Hispanic Voter Project, at Johns Hopkins University, the Bush campaign poured money into Florida media markets in particular, stoking Hispanic anger over the Clinton Administration's handling of the Elián González affair—and ultimately helping to deprive Gore of the state and the election. (In contrast, Gore outspent Bush nearly three to one in New Mexico, and won.) And with some strategists believing that the 2004 election, too, could hinge on Florida—and that Florida could hinge on the heavily Hispanic I-4 corridor between Tampa and Orlando— the Democrats are sure to avoid making the same mistake again.

The Upper Midwest. The culturally cautious Rust Belt states that were a key to Bush's win have been particularly hard hit by the net loss of 3 million jobs since Bush took office, 2.4 million of them in the manufacturing sector. As the Democratic contenders delight in pointing out, Bush stands to become the first President since Herbert Hoover to see the country lose more jobs than it gained on his watch. Even if the economy improves, a critical component of the Democrats' regional rhetoric will be reminding voters exactly how many manufacturing jobs have been lost in states such as Michigan (127,000), Pennsylvania (132,500), and Ohio (151,800).

The Mississippi Basin. Finally, for all the ribbing it drew, Gore's four-day riverboat tour along the Mississippi after the Democratic convention is likely to be repeated in some fashion by the next Democratic nominee. Though Bush's campaign manager, Karl Rove, dismissed it at the time as a corny gimmick, he later changed his mind. By floating down the river Gore hit small, difficult-to-reach media markets in such key midwestern swing states as Minnesota, Wisconsin, Illinois, Iowa, and Missouri. (He won all but Missouri.) When Rove later sought to target some of these same areas, he discovered that no airport nearby was large enough to land the Boeing 757 that served as Bush's campaign plane. "We never got Bush there," Rove lamented afterward, and he laid the blame for Gore's narrow win in Iowa on that fact.

If the 2000 election supplied the road map for the next campaign, the 2002 midterm elections gave both parties an urgent mandate to reach swing voters. Democratic campaigns mostly outperformed their Republican counterparts in the elections of 1996, 1998, and 2000. (Gore did, after all, win more votes than any U.S. President except Reagan.) This was thanks largely to Election Day voter-turnout efforts, which got Democrats to the polls and often proved decisive. But in 2002 the Republicans shocked the Democrats by besting them on this front, nullifying an important edge. This has set off a pitched battle to capture the narrowing sliver of what pollsters call "persuadables"—the undecided voters who will make the difference in any close election.

> *Latinos ... now represent an important swing vote.*

In fact, it has sparked a kind of demographic arms race. For the first time, both parties are embracing sophisticated and costly demographic technology that until recently was the province of consumer market-research companies. The Democratic National Committee has acquired a database of 158 million voters it has dubbed the "DataMart." Appended to every name are as many as 306 "lifestyle variables" gleaned from voter files, consumer databases, and other sources. From these, candidates can find out a citizen's voting record, number of children, kind of car, favorite television shows and magazines, and even number of pets. Not to be outdone, the Republican National Committee has its own Orwellian construct, called the "Voter Vault," which contains records on 165 million people.

By drawing samples from the DataMart, the thinking goes, Democratic pollsters and interest groups can create intricate predictive models of where the most sought-after voters will be found. "In a crowded marketplace," the pollster Geoff Garin explains, "it's about being able to know the architecture of the people most likely to be supportive of you and seeking them out."

It is no longer enough to posit that a broad notional category such as "soccer moms" will decide an election. Advances in computer and database technology now offer infinitely more detail, promising campaign staffs the capacity to learn not only which issues matter most to a particular soccer mom but also her home address, the phrasing likeliest to persuade her, and when, how, and by whom she might prefer to be approached. Karen White, the political director for the pro-choice women's group EMILY'S List, which is working with DataMart information, says, "In the past we've always tried to bring voters to us on our issues. This time we're getting so much insight into their personal lives that we can actually bring what they need to hear to them, on their terms."

The New Democrat Network, a centrist political organization, was among the first in this election cycle to use polling to sketch out a profile of the latest generation of swing voters. Data shared with each of the Democratic candidates (and provided to *The Atlantic*) describes them as mainly white and also younger, less likely to vote, and more likely than self-identified Democrats or Republicans to characterize themselves as "workaholics." They are most heavily concentrated in suburbs and small cities, and though they disapprove of many Bush Administration policies, they tend to be more religious and to admire military service more than most Democrats do. "On many issues their attitudes correspond strongly with the Democratic Party even though demographically they are closer to Republican voters," says Peter Brodnitz, of the firm Penn, Schoen and Berland, which conducted the poll. The New Democrat Network identified civil liberties and the environment as the two issues on which independents and Republicans most strongly disagree—and, indeed, many of the Democratic candidates have sounded precisely these themes. (Buried in the report's "tactical recommendations" is information that both sides in the next campaign may find useful: independents listen to a disproportionate amount of country radio, and they watch *SportsCenter* more often than other Americans—a taste, the poll reveals, that corresponds more closely with Democrats' than Republicans.')

Other organizations, including Emily's List, have conducted broader studies to sort independents into smaller "lifestyle clusters," the better to target them in the fall. EMILY'S List has identified four basic groups: disengaged "Bystanders," who when motivated to vote lean Democratic; "Senior Health Care" voters, whose gender (predominantly female) suggests an inclination to support Democrats; "Education First" voters, 64 percent female and 66 percent pro-choice but currently more supportive of Bush and the Iraq War than the typical Democrat; and the "Young Economically Pressured," many of whom work more than 40 hours a week and may care for an elderly parent. Though this last group tends to support the Democratic position on funding public schools and other issues, its members live predominantly in small towns or rural areas and are culturally conservative. The challenge for the next Democratic candidate will be reaching all these independents, many of whom live in small cities and suburbs that are gradually abandoning the Democratic Party. The suburban vote, which Bush won narrowly in 2000, continues to grow. Suburban women already tend to vote Democratic, so the nominee must make a special effort to appeal to men, whose vote fluctuates more than women's in presidential elections and who have lately deserted the party in large numbers: men now prefer Republicans over Democrats by 19 percentage points. Efforts to do this are under way on gun control and other issues. Gore was widely thought to have lost blue-collar swing voters in West Virginia and Ohio because of his position on guns and—pollsters argue—how he spoke about it: gun owners believed that Gore would take away their weapons, and voted accordingly. But pollsters discovered that if the discussion had simply been reframed to acknowledge the Second Amendment right to bear arms (as in the phrase "with rights come responsibilities"), 20 percent of gun owners—seven percent of the electorate—would have been inclined to vote Democratic. It's probably no accident that none of the leading Democratic candidates have echoed Gore.

> *Values . . . have replaced income as the best indicator of voting behavior.*

One early lesson that ought to figure in the Democratic campaign is the importance of values, which have replaced income as the best indicator of voting behavior. In the past income corresponded strongly to party preference: voters supported the Democratic Party when they were poor and grew increasingly Republican as they moved up the income scale. That's no longer true. The exodus of white working-class voters from the Democratic Party has been well documented ever since the Republican revolution of 1994. A similar migration away from the Republican Party by affluent suburbanites alienated by the party's social conservatism has received less notice. Just as white working-class voters swung Georgia and other once Democratic states to the Republican Party, affluent suburbanites turned formerly Republican states such as Illinois and New Jersey into Democratic strongholds. The Democratic nominee will have to hold on to these upscale voters while winning back working-class voters.

"We're a party that prefers to talk about issues, not values," says Bruce Reed, who was Bill Clinton's domestic-policy chief. "Clinton demonstrated that if we want to expand our reach, we have to talk in terms of values." Clinton successfully rewrote the language of values to fit his own policies—family and medical leave, the V-chip, school uniforms—rather than those of the social conservatives who popularized it. In fact, both Clinton and Bush set an example for the next Democratic nominee by rising above party stereotype to attract independents: Clinton by endorsing fiscal conservatism, fighting crime, and opposing welfare dependency; Bush by using enough compassionate rhetoric to persuade independents that he wasn't another meanspirited Republican like Newt Gingrich.

It is a rare point of agreement among Democrats that the party owes its win in the 2000 popular vote to an unprecedented mobilization of minority and union voters. Any serious discussion of another close election must be premised on a similar performance. The strong Republican turnout efforts in the 2002 and 2003 elections have only increased the pressure on the next Democratic campaign to keep pace.

One way Democrats hope to do so is by improving their methods of reaching voters. Party bosses once relied on local precinct captains to impart a measure of personalization to even the largest campaigns. In the 1970s and 1980s, however, television developed into a more efficient medium; direct human contact waned, eventually giving rise to the maddening wall-to-wall carpet-bombing of TV attack ads that are the hallmark of modern campaigns. Today, in light of the proven benefits of voter-turnout efforts, strategists in both parties are hoping to combine demographic information with political research in order to repersonalize campaigns and lure back dropout voters who are disillusioned with politics. EMILY'S List has even asked voters in certain elections to keep a diary of every political contact they received, recording each instance in which a television ad, phone call, or direct-mail brochure caught their attention.

Perhaps most striking about the Democratic effort to shape the next campaign is its urgency. The McCain-Feingold campaign-finance-reform laws have had the effect of directing much of the available campaign money away from the Democratic National Committee and toward a broad range of liberal interest groups. Within these groups there is a palpable sense of desperation about the party's predicament and a corresponding willingness to experiment that the hidebound DNC rarely displayed. There is also the stinging example of Karl Rove, who brilliantly understood that rigorously pursuing a patchwork of distinct constituencies could add up to an unlikely electoral victory. But above all there is the pervasive fear that the next Democratic candidate will once again be a hairsbreadth from victory—and once again manage to lose.

Where the Swing Voters Live

Using categories created by Claritas, a market-research company, the polling firm Penn, Schoen and Berland has identified the three "social groups" that will make up the swing vote in the 2004 election.

- **Elite Suburbs:** Members of this group—which is predominantly white with significant concentrations of Asian-Americans—have six-figure incomes (from managerial and professional jobs), postgraduate degrees, and large homes. They tend to buy expensive clothes and luxury cars, and to travel abroad.

- **Second-city Society:** These are the wealthiest families who have settled in metropolitan areas outside urban cores. Most are married couples with children; they have college degrees and executive jobs, and they spend heavily on digital and wireless technology, casual dining restaurants, upscale retail goods, and luxury cars.

- **Rustic Living:** The members of this group live in isolated towns and rural villages. They have modest incomes, low levels of education, and blue-collar jobs. The young singles and senior citizens who make up this group spend their leisure time hunting and fishing, attending social activities at local churches and veterans' clubs, listening to country music, and watching auto races.

New Generation, New Politics[5]

By Anna Greenberg
The American Prospect, October 1, 2003

A new generation is coming of age in America and politicians
ignore it at their peril. Generation Y, as it's been called, is expected
to be as large as the Baby Boom Generation, and when the full
group is of voting age, it could have as much political significance. It
is a generation that has thus far shown itself to be disdainful of politics, cynical about political parties, and more likely than any other
age group to support third-party candidates. At the same time,
these young people are engaged in the life of the community and
expect to improve it. To write them off politically is to risk someone
else mobilizing a sleeping giant.

But reaching Generation Y voters will take some doing. They have
little interest in retirement security or reforming Medicare, the
dominant political issues of the last few election cycles. They are a
racially diverse and, in many ways, a politically progressive group;
as a result, more of them call themselves Democrats than do their
predecessors in Generation X and even the Baby Boom Generation.
But their political worldview contains a complicated mix of liberal
and conservative perspectives. Either Democrats or Republicans
could plausibly win broad favor with this generation, but only if
they can find the right message and deliver it with authenticity in a
medium that young people are tuned to.

Political professionals usually dismiss Generation Y because it
votes at a much lower rate than older Americans. Yet even at this
depressed rate, voters under 25 years old will constitute between 7
percent and 8 percent of the electorate in 2004. They will rival in
size other coveted swing groups such as "soccer moms" and "office-
park dads." More important, they are the future electorate.

The Long Goodbye

The young voters of Generation Y in many ways represent the cul-
mination of years of disaffection with politics and traditional political institutions. Their grandparents or great-grandparents are the
Silent generation, the electorate's strongest partisans whose enduring ties to the Democratic Party were forged during the Franklin D.
Roosevelt years and the formation of the modern welfare state.
These seniors grew up at the height of civic engagement and collective community in America, buying war bonds, saving rubber bands,

---

the oldest of them serving overseas. And as study after study has demonstrated, they continue to participate in politics at much higher rates than their progeny. (Because generations are rough categories, defined with different cutoff dates by different researchers—and because voting and polling results are often reported not by genera-tion at all but by other age groupings—the data are not tidy. Nonetheless the overall picture is unmistakable.)

> *Generation X . . . remains the most disaffected—and conservative—in the electorate.*

Partisan allegiance weak-ened among the next generation, the baby boomers, as young peo-ple challenged traditional institutions and social mores during the civil-rights, anti-war, and women's movements. Participation in electoral politics remained relatively high in 1972, when 50 per-cent of baby boomers—those under 25 years of age—voted in the presidential election. But the subsequent fallout from the Vietnam War and the Watergate scandal marked them with a growing dis-trust of government and political leadership.

The children of the baby boomers, Generation X, were thus born into a world of increasing cynicism about government, and they grew up during the Ronald Reagan and George Bush Senior administrations, when government was under systematic assault and social ills were blamed on a failed welfare state. Their depressed outlook was further fueled by a multitude of griefs— from rising divorce rates to the economic recession to the crack epi-demic to the AIDS explosion—that made the world a dangerous place. In 1984 and 1988, as Generation X came of voting age, only 40.8 percent and 36.2 percent of people under 25 voted in those respective presidential elections. And this generation remains the most disaffected—and conservative—in the electorate.

Today's youngest voters, Generation Y, were raised during the heady 1990s, a time of seemingly endless dotcom possibilities, as well as social projects such as AmeriCorps that were championed by the nation's political leadership. Volunteer programs blossomed and flourished on college and high-school campuses. (As Robert Putnam shows in *Bowling Alone*, the rise of American volunteer-ism since 1975 is due solely to increases among the senior citizens of the most civically engaged generation and among people born after 1975.) But these more optimistic times did not generate any more interest in electoral politics. Just 32 percent of voters under 25 participated in the 2000 presidential election, even lower than the turnout of Gen Xers at the same age.

The Republican Surge

It is a staple of political science that people's political identities are largely formed in their youths—and are influenced not just by their families, schools, and religious institutions but also by the political times in which they come of age. Moreover, studies show that these influences endure. As Warren E. Miller and J. Merrill Shanks demonstrate in *The New American Voter*, the percentage of Democrats and Republicans in the electorate changes over time largely because one generation dies out and another enters, not because contemporary events alter party identifications across generations.

Thus, the recession and economic insecurity that Gen Xers faced in their early 20s, as well as 12 years of Republican administrations, left behind a cohort that entered the Republican camp in droves in the 1980s and stayed there. In 2000, according to the University of Michigan's National Election Study, only 26 percent of voters between 30 and 39 years old (mostly Gen X voters) called themselves Democrats, making them the least Democratic sector of the electorate. Survey data collected by Democracy Corps, a Democratic polling and strategy group, show the same patterns. (See chart below.)

Generation Y, however, halted these trends toward Republicanism fairly decisively. According to the National Election Study, only 18 percent of voters under 30 called themselves Republicans in 2000, compared with 35 percent of voters aged 30 to 39. Exit polls show that in 1984, with the first Gen Xers reaching the voting booths, 59 percent of voters under 30 supported Reagan. By 2000, as Generation Y began to vote, 53 percent of voters under 30 voted for Al Gore or Ralph Nader, compared with 50 percent of voters ages 30 to 44.

It is important to note that the move away from the Republican Party is driven, in part, by the nation's growing racial diversity. Only 67 percent of Gen Y voters are white, and that has a profound effect on the generation's partisanship. African American and Latino voters are significantly more likely to identify themselves as Democrats and support Democratic candidates than white voters. Fully 90 percent of African Americans and 67 percent of Latino voters supported Gore in the 2000 presidential election.

At the same time, as the Democracy Corps data shows, Gen Y voters are more likely than any other generation to call themselves independents. According to the National Election Study, nearly 47 percent of voters under 30 called themselves independents in 2000. Trends in voting for third-party candidates confirmed it. In 1998,

Partisan Identification by Generation

	Gen Y	Gen X	Boomers	Silent	GI
Democrat	38%	36%	37%	39%	39%
Independent	29	25	27	24	20
Republican	33	38	35	36	41
Net D-R	+5	-2	+2	+3	-2

Source: Democracy Corps, 2001–2002

Jesse Ventura won 46 percent of the under-30 vote, compared with 29 percent among older voters. In 2000, Nader received 5 percent of the vote from those under 30, compared with 2 percent among voters over 30 years of age.

The View from the 20s

These numbers reflect a complicated worldview. The youngest generation of voters is cynical about politics but attracted to independent candidates.

The youngest generation of voters is cynical about politics but attracted to independent candidates.

It leans Democratic, unlike Generation X, but its attitudes do not neatly mirror the agenda that has developed in the Democratic—or, for that matter, the Republican—Party. In fact, its mix of liberal and conservative perspectives do not map neatly onto any party's current platform.

For example, younger voters hold more expansive notions about the responsibilities of government than do older voters; at the same time, they are very individualistic about problem solving and supportive of market solutions. These seemingly contradictory views reflect a national narrative in the 1990s that included Bill Clinton's progressive vision of the role of government in people's lives and the country's simultaneous insistence that we end "welfare as we know it."

Almost 70 percent of voters under 30 support bigger government over smaller government, and nearly two-thirds of young people between 15 and 25 years of age think that government should do more to solve people's problems.

Nonetheless, young people support the privatization of Social Security, private health insurance for prescription drugs, and school vouchers. The data suggest that young people generally want government to "care," but they do not have well-developed ideas about how that might work.

The nation's youngest voters are by far its most socially liberal voters. For instance, 72 percent of those between 18 and 24 agree that there should be "laws that provide gay and lesbian couples who form civil unions the same legal rights as married couples when it comes to things like inheritance, employer-provided health insurance, and hospital visits." More than half of adults under 30 think that gays and lesbians should have a legal right to get married, compared with just 37 percent of baby boomers and 20 percent of seniors. Younger voters are also more supportive of affirmative action than the rest of the electorate and hold a more positive view of immigrants.

But this liberalism is not necessarily tied to other social issues. It does not translate into more support for abortion rights, feminism, or relaxed sexual mores. People under 30 are no more pro-choice than their predecessors who fought for abortion rights in the '60s and '70s. Unlike the Baby Boom Generation, which linked many issues such as civil rights, abortion choice, women's rights, and sexual freedom into a coherent agenda, Gen Y is untroubled by simultaneous expressions of open-mindedness and traditionalism.

The Youth Agenda

While everyone bemoans the fact that young people do not participate in politics, neither major party has done much to reach out to them. In the last three election cycles, the Democrats have focused on seniors' issues such as retirement security and prescription drugs. It is remarkable that the party has maintained an edge with young voters given this utter disconnection from them. The Republican Party's emphasis on tax cuts has tapped into a concern of young people (especially those without a college education), but its stances on gay rights and the environment have been fundamentally at odds with young voters' values.

Both parties have largely chosen to communicate the same, older-

---

While everyone bemoans the fact that young people do not participate in politics, neither major party has done much to reach out to them.

---

oriented message to all voters. But young voters have a different set of concerns than their elders. For instance, everyone is worried about the economy, but older people feel the recession in the declining value of their 401(k)s and the rising cost of health insurance; the young, meanwhile, worry about job security and wages. Some 15.6 percent of people between ages 18 and 24 are currently without jobs, compared with 6.4 percent in the total population, and unemployment rates are skyrocketing among minority youth.

Young voters' concerns about education—consistently one of their top interests—are also distinct. They support more funding and smaller class sizes for grades K–12, but they also are having a difficult time paying for college, whether that means a four-year bachelor's degree from a prestigious university or an associate's degree from a community college. The need to work while in school and the later burden of paying off student loans put an enormous financial strain on the many young people whose parents can't foot the full bill. Today's rising tuitions, the less generous federal loan policies embedded in the new tax code and the cuts in state budgets for higher education can only exacerbate this situation.

Generation Y also places a higher priority on environmental issues than older voters. Significantly more young people—especially young men—oppose drilling in the Arctic National Wildlife Refuge in Alaska, for example, than older voters, and they are more likely to say that protecting the environment is more important than developing new sources of energy and encouraging economic growth.

There is a populist, progressive agenda that could reflect young people's core values and priorities—and, indeed, lend them some coherence. It would call on government to actively provide opportunities for people to acquire the skills and resources they need to succeed in life. It would not, however, encourage dependence on government but instead offer the means for self-improvement and self-reliance. Such a platform would call for individuals to take personal responsibility for their behavior, government to protect the earth's natural resources, and society to be open to difference and diversity.

But there is also a conservative agenda that might win over Generation Y. This platform would invoke personal responsibility in matters economic, as well as sexual. It would emphasize what government takes away from individuals (tax dollars, for instance) and the role markets might play in solving their problems. Certainly conservatives would have to be mindful of the racial diversity and social liberalism of this generation, but these young voters are not beyond their reach.

For the moment, Generation Y has stopped the national slide into Republicanism and offers a more optimistic and open view of the future. But politically it remains very much up for grabs—and adrift in a political culture that offers stale political leadership and old ways of talking about politics. In a country split 50-50 politically, the side that successfully speaks to this generation may well be the side that wins.

A Better Ballot?[6]

By Mary Wiltenburg
The Christian Science Monitor, November 3, 2003

When voters head to the polls Tuesday, those using punch-card ballots—notorious for their role in the 2000 presidential election recount—may do so with a lingering unease that their votes could go uncounted. Others will enter sleek new electronic voting booths bought at great price by a patchwork of states and counties trying to guard against butterfly ballots and hanging chads.

But a growing number of computer scientists are now warning that the new technology, far from solving America's voting problems, may actually make things worse. Electronic ballots can be miscounted too, they say—or the machines that tally them tampered with and traces of sabotage erased.

"If you look at the consequences for democracy, it's terrifying," says David Dill, a Stanford University computer-science professor who has led the charge to raise awareness about the machines' potential security flaws. "If we had a way to make [computerized voting] safe, believe me, we would. There's no way to run a reliable election without a verifiable paper trail—that's what these machines don't have."

Others, including makers of the electronic systems and politicians who tout them, argue that democracy always has been a messy process and that no technology is foolproof. As long as there's been a vote, they say, there have been ballots destroyed, misread, and counterfeited; machines worn out or sabotaged; officials bribed; voters bullied or denied their rights. Some disabled citizens have been unable to vote privately, illiterates have been unable to vote knowingly, and voters with limited English have not understood how to cast ballots that count. Electronic voting is the latest in a long line of imperfect solutions, its proponents say, but it's the best option there is.

Voting was a matter of assessing shouts and shows of hands back in Colonial days. In the 1770s, these unverifiable counts were replaced by ballots written longhand, which left a paper trail but took a long time to tally. In 1892, self-tallying lever machines sped up the process, but again left no paper record. When punch-card ballots hit the scene in the 1960s, jurisdictions began to replace the old lever machines. But the punch-card system had its own weaknesses.

---

6. By Mary Wiltenburg. This article first appeared in *The Christian Science Monitor* on November 3, 2003, and is reproduced with permission. Copyright © 2003 The Christian Science Monitor (*www.csmonitor.com*). All rights reserved.

Even before the 2000 Florida fiasco, some states had switched to the mark-sense or optical-scan ballots, which are much like fill-in-the-bubble standardized tests.

After the recount debacle, officials scrambled to ensure that no future chads would be left hanging. Congress passed the Help America Vote Act of 2002 (HAVA), but has so far supplied only $664.5 million to fund it. So solutions have come in fits and starts, with counties adopting a hodgepodge of systems. Last November, Georgia became the first state to install touch-screen machines at all its polling stations, under a $54 million contract with Diebold Election Systems, a supplier of Direct Recording Electronic voting systems (DREs).

Many Georgia voters were impressed. Kim Hullett, who used a new model in Fayette County's latest election, says the machines—which work much like automatic teller machines—were easy to understand, kept lines moving, and meant she and her husband could track election results on the Web as they heard about them on the TV news.

But Professor Dill, at Stanford, had doubts. A concerned activist had sent him a copy of the Diebold system's source code—the road map to its computer voting software—which the company had been storing on a publicly accessible server. Diebold says this code was partial and outdated. Dill gave the code to a team of computer security experts led by Avi Rubin, technical director of the Information Security Institute at Johns Hopkins University.

The team's report, released in July, marked the first time any company's voting-system software has been publicly evaluated by an academic team. Over 24 pages, it details what Dr. Rubin describes as system-security flaws the average teenager today would be computer-savvy enough to exploit.

Two big flaws, Rubin says, could give rise to any number of nightmare scenarios. The first: The machines' software is encrypted in only the most basic ways, so people with access to a machine before Election Day could easily get into it and, for instance, change the program so that all votes for one candidate go to an opponent. The second: Diebold machines, like comparable machines sold by Sequoia Voting Systems and Election Systems & Software, produce no paper record of a vote, making recounts impossible. A computer science professor, Rubin says he's all in favor of computerizing needless paperwork—but sometimes, in the interest of democracy, you need to kill a few trees.

Diebold rebutted the team's report, arguing it failed to take into account all the checks and balances that ensure election security. Rubin's team argued back that poll workers cannot be expected to make up for security flaws in election machines.

Caught in the crossfire, Maryland put on hold a $55.6 million contract with Diebold to outfit the entire state, and asked Scientific Applications International Corp., an independent research firm, to investigate. Though the firm's report cautiously confirmed some of the Rubin team's findings, it said many flaws could be corrected, and Maryland decided to go ahead with the purchase. Last month, two lawmakers requested a further review of the matter by an independent state agency.

Meanwhile, states are in limbo—awaiting word on the security of DRE machines before spending more on them, as well as late-arriving HAVA funding. The 2002 act mandates numerous state and county reforms, such as establishing reliable voter rolls (many African-Americans were mistakenly cut from Florida's 2000 eligible-voter lists, and in Denver last month, nearly 200 deceased voters were invited to cast absentee ballots).

The law does not require states to install electronic systems, but the technology holds appeal because of its flexibility, says Roy Saltman, a private election-technology consultant. DREs can give instructions in many languages, and can be adapted for visually impaired voters. HAVA requires that all new systems and safeguards be in place by January 2006, a deadline many states expect to miss.

Critics and some proponents of DREs agree on one thing: the need for a paper audit trail so votes can be recounted. A bill now before Congress would add that requirement.

From Quill to Touch Screen: A U.S. History of Ballot-Casting

- 1770s: Balloting replaces a show of hands or voice votes. Voters write out names of their candidates in longhand, and give their ballots to an election judge.
- 1850s: Political parties disperse preprinted lists of candidates, enabling the illiterate to vote. The ballot becomes a long strip of paper, like a railroad ticket.
- 1869: Thomas Edison receives a patent for his invention of the voting machine, intended for counting congressional votes.
- 1888: Massachusetts prints a ballot, at public expense, listing names of all candidates nominated and their party affiliation. Most states adopt this landmark improvement within eight years.
- 1892: A lever-operated voting machine is first used at a Lockport, N.Y., town meeting. Similar machines are still in use today.
- 1964: A punch-card ballot is introduced in two counties in Georgia. Almost 4 in 10 voters used punch cards in the 1996 presidential election.
- 1990s: Michigan is the first to switch to optical scanning, used for decades in standardized testing. One-quarter of voters used the technology in the 1996 election.
- 2000: A storm erupts over Florida's punch-card ballots and Palm Beach County's "butterfly ballot" in the presidential election.
- 2002: New federal law authorizes $3.9 billion over three years to help states upgrade voting technologies and phase out punch cards and lever machines. Georgia is the first state to use DRE touch-screen technology exclusively.

Sources: Federal Elections Commission; "Elections A to Z," *CQ*, 2003; *International Encyclopedia of Elections*, CQ Press, 2000; League of Women Voters

Voting-Machine Makers to Fight Security Criticism[7]

BY JONATHAN KRIM
THE WASHINGTON POST, DECEMBER 9, 2003

Electronic-voting-machine companies announced yesterday that they are banding together to counter mounting concerns about whether their machines are secure enough to withstand tampering by hackers.

Although less than 20 percent of the nation's counties use electronic voting machines, their use is growing in the wake of the problems with punch-card ballots in Florida that threw the 2000 presidential election into turmoil. Last year Congress passed the Help America Vote Act, which provides funds for states and localities to modernize their election systems.

But several academic and cyber-security experts argue that the new machines, which let voters make their choices on video screens, have disturbing security flaws.

In July, researchers at Johns Hopkins University and Rice University identified potential security holes that would allow vote tampering in systems made by industry leader Diebold Election Systems Inc.

That report led Maryland state officials to delay purchasing $55 million in systems from Diebold, although Gov. Robert L. Ehrlich Jr. (R) ultimately decided to move ahead.

Critics argue that at minimum, the machines should be equipped to provide companion paper records of the votes as a check against simple malfunctions, someone commandeering the operating systems and voting multiple times, or causing others' votes to be lost.

Last month California said it would require a paper verification system.

The leading voting-machine companies, which argue that their systems are safe, have yet to put forward any proposals on addressing the concerns. But under the umbrella leadership of the Information Technology Association of America, the industry hopes to foster conversation that includes security experts, academics, local elections officials, and the National Institute of Standards and Technology, the federal agency overseeing technical standards.

---

7. © 2003, *The Washington Post*, reprinted with permission.

"This is an inflection point in the history of voting in this country," said Harris N. Miller, president of the IT association and a former Democratic Party chairman in Fairfax County. "There's a certain amount of controversy . . . the companies have decided they want to deal with that controversy positively."

Bill Stotesbery, vice president of Hart InterCivic Inc., which has 25,000 machines in use in Virginia and several other states, said the electronic voting systems are not connected to the Internet, which would be a prime avenue for hackers.

He said his company and others have the capability to provide printed verification of an individual's vote, which would at least allow the voter to determine whether the machine properly recorded his or her choices.

But he said that many local jurisdictions have not yet demanded such a capability, nor have they prescribed technical standards. Paper printers could add $500 to the cost of each machine.

But the Johns Hopkins study, and others, said the systems could be compromised by preprogrammed "smart cards" that each voter uses to activate the machines, or other tampering.

Security experts also worry about mischievous insiders at the voting-machine companies. That fear was fanned when Walden W. O'Dell, chief executive of Diebold Inc., told Republicans in an Aug. 14 fundraising letter that he is "committed to helping Ohio deliver its electoral votes to the president."

The company also has angered critics by suing two Swarthmore College students who posted on the Internet internal Diebold memos indicating the company's awareness of security flaws.

A Diebold spokesman said the firm has dropped the legal action.

II. The Two-Party System

Editor's Introduction

T hroughout history people with common interests have joined together to form political factions and parties to promote their agendas. Each democratic nation has developed its own unique party system: Some countries have only one viable party, while others have quite a few. In the United States, soon after the Constitution was ratified, a two-party system quickly emerged that has endured to this day and remains a vital aspect of American elections.

The two factions that first sprouted following the adoption of the Constitution in 1788 were the Federalists of John Adams and Alexander Hamilton and the Democratic-Republicans of Thomas Jefferson and James Madison. The Federalist Party petered out after 20 years or so, but the Democratic-Republicans became one of the most successful and enduring political organizations in history, evolving into the modern-day Democratic Party. More than 200 years after its inception, the Democratic Party remains one half of America's two-party system.

Following the demise of the Federalists, the Whig Party became the primary alternative to the Democrats, thus ensuring the integrity of the two-party system. In the decades that followed, the Whig Party lost its hold over the electorate and, like the Federalist Party before it, disintegrated. In 1856, however, new life was breathed into the two-party system when the Republican Party, also known today as the Grand Old Party (GOP), ran its first presidential candidate and soon challenged the Democrats for national supremacy.

Since the rise of the GOP, American politics has been dominated by the struggle between the Democrats and Republicans. The first selection in this chapter, excerpted from *Wikipedia*, explains how the two major parties initially developed and how radically they have changed over the years. A piece by Ted Halstead for the *Atlantic Monthly* examines the two parties as they are today, analyzing the make-up of their adherents and the policy positions they support. Halstead duly highlights each party's internal contradictions and overall weaknesses as well. In a more personal look at the parties and their members, Elisabeth Rosenthal for the *New York Times* profiles Al Puchala and Douglas Korn, two political novices who recently became committed party activists and fund-raisers. A Democratic convert, Puchala joined the party in response to what he perceived as the irresponsible fiscal and foreign policy of President George W. Bush, while Korn joined the ranks of the GOP in large measure because he supported the president's stated goal of democratizing the Middle East.

Despite the duopoly on political power maintained by the Democrats and Republicans over the last 150 years or so, third parties, though they have never captured the White House, have made notable contributions to the national discourse and have decisively influenced election results. Jim Eskin, in a piece for the *San Antonio Business Journal*, takes a broad look at third parties throughout American history and concludes that though the groups themselves may have failed at the polls, oftentimes their positions were coopted and implemented by the major parties so that, in the end, their goals were achieved. Frequently, however, third parties meet with decidedly mixed results; in this regard, Bree Hocking, for *Roll Call*, chronicles the recent tribulations of the Reform Party. Founded by H. Ross Perot following his impressive showing in the 1992 presidential election, the Reform Party has since fallen on difficult times and faces dwindling membership rolls and ideological uncertainty.

United States Political Parties[1]

WIKIPEDIA, 2004

Democratic Party

The Democratic Party is a United States political party. From 1833 to 1856, it was opposed chiefly by the Whig Party. From 1856 onward its main opposition has come from the Republican Party.

The Democratic National Committee (DNC) of the United States provides national leadership for the United States Democratic Party. It is responsible for developing and promoting the Democratic political platform, as well as coordinating fundraising and election strategy. There are similar committees in every U.S. state and most U.S. Counties (though in some states, party organization lower than state-level is arranged by legislative districts). It can be considered the counterpart of the Republican National Committee. Its current chair is Terry McAuliffe.

On January 15, 1870, a political cartoon appearing in *Harper's Weekly* titled "A Live Jackass Kicking a Dead Lion" by Thomas Nast, for the first time symbolized the Democratic Party as a donkey. Since then, the donkey has been widely used as a symbol of the party, though unlike the Republican elephant, the donkey has never been officially adopted as the party's logo.

History

The Democratic Party traces its origin to the Democratic-Republican Party founded by Thomas Jefferson in 1793. The Democratic Party itself was formed from a faction of the Democratic-Republicans, led by Andrew Jackson. Following his defeat in the election of 1824 despite having a majority of the popular vote, Andrew Jackson set about building a political coalition strong enough to defeat John Quincy Adams in the election of 1828. The coalition that he built was the foundation of the subsequent Democratic Party.

In the 1850s, following the disintegration of the Whig Party, the southern wing of the Democratic Party became increasingly associated with the continuation and expansion of slavery, in opposition of the newly formed Republican Party. Democrats in the northern states opposed this new trend, and at the 1860 nominating convention the party split and nominated two candidates. As a result, the Democrats went down in defeat—part of the chain of events lead-

---

1. This article is licensed under the Free Documentation License. It uses material from the *Wikipedia* articles "Democratic Party" and "Republican Party."

ing up to the Civil War. After the war, the Democrats were a shattered party, but eventually gathered enough support to elect reform candidate Grover Cleveland to two terms in the presidency.

In 1896 the Democrats chose William Jennings Bryan over Cleveland as their candidate, who then lost to William McKinley. The Democrats did not regain the presidency until Taft and Roosevelt split the Republican vote and Woodrow Wilson won with a modest plurality in 1912. The Republicans again took the lead in 1920 by championing laissez-faire regulatory policies. The stock market crash in 1929 and the ensuing Great Depression set the stage for a more interventionist government and Franklin Delano Roosevelt (FDR) won a landslide election in 1932, campaigning on a platform of "relief, recovery, and reform."

FDR's New Deal programs focused on job-creation through public works projects as well as on social welfare programs such as Social Security. The political coalition of labor unions, minorities, liberals, and southern whites (the New Deal Coalition) allowed the Demo-

---

The Democrats are generally a catch-all party with widespread appeal to most opponents of the Republicans.

---

crats to control the government for much of the next 30 years, until the issue of civil rights divided conservative southern whites from the rest of the party.

The political pendulum swung away from the Democrats with the election of Republican president Ronald Reagan in 1980. By 1980 the country was ready for a change in political vision after a decade of poor economic performance and several embarrassments abroad including the Vietnam War and the Iranian hostage crisis at the end of the Carter presidency. Riding on Reagan's coattails, the Republican Party successfully positioned itself as the party of national strength, gaining 34 seats in the House and gaining control of the Senate for the first time since 1955.

The Democratic Leadership Council organized by elected Democratic leaders has in recent years worked to position the Party towards a centrist position. It still retains a powerful base of left-of-center supporters, however, as like the Republicans, the Democrats are generally a catch-all party with widespread appeal to most opponents of the Republicans. This includes organized labour, educators, environmentalists, gays, pro-choicers, and other opponents of the social conservatism practiced by many Republicans.

In the 1990s the Democratic Party re-invigorated itself by providing a successful roadmap to economic growth. Led by Bill Clinton, the Democrats championed a balanced federal budget and job growth through a strong economy. Labor unions, which had been steadily losing membership since the 1960s, found they had also lost political clout inside the Democratic Party: Clinton enacted the NAFTA free trade agreement with Canada and Mexico over the strong objection of the unions.

In the 2000 Presidential election the party's left wing splintered somewhat under the candidacy of Al Gore. Some former Democratic voters felt the party was becoming too centrist, and moving away from its traditional ways of political liberalism and progressivism. The left-wing Green Party candidate Ralph Nader in turn managed to take many votes away from Al Gore in many traditionally liberal states an event which is often cited as one of the leading causes of Al Gore's narrow defeat.

Since the September 11, 2001 Terrorist Attacks, the Democrats have been faced with a new political puzzle as the nation's focus has now changed to issues of national security and homeland security, with the Democrats positioning themselves against war in Iraq and advocating a less aggressive policy.

Republican Party

Republican party logo, adopted in the 1970's, depicts a stylized elephant in red, white, and blue.

The Republican Party (often GOP for Grand Old Party) is a United States political party that was organized in Jackson, Michigan, on February 28, 1854, as a party against the expansion of slavery. It is not to be confused with the Democratic-Republican Party of Thomas Jefferson or the National Republican Party of Henry Clay. The first convention of the U.S. Republican Party was held on July 6, 1854, in Jackson, Michigan. Many of its initial policies were inspired by the defunct Whig Party. Since its inception, its chief opponent has been the Democratic Party.

The Republican National Committee (RNC) of the United States provides national leadership for the United States Republican Party. It is responsible for developing and promoting the Republican political platform, as well as coordinating fundraising and election strategy. There are similar committees in every U.S. state and most U.S. Counties (though in some states, party organization lower than state-level is arranged by legislative districts). It can be considered the counterpart of the Democratic National Committee. The chairman of the RNC, since July, 2003, is Ed Gillespie.

The official symbol of the Republican Party is the elephant. Although the elephant had occasionally been associated with the party earlier, a cartoon by Thomas Nast, published in *Harper's Weekly* on November 7, 1874, is considered the first important use of the symbol.

History

John C. Frémont ran as the first Republican for President in 1856, using the political slogan: "Free soil, free labor, free speech, free men, Frémont." The party grew especially rapidly in Northeastern and Midwestern states, where slavery had long been prohibited, culminating in a sweep of victories in the Northern states and the election of Lincoln in 1860, ending 60 years of dominance by Southern Democrats and ushering in a new era of Republican dominance based in the industrial north.

With the end of the Civil War came the upheavals of Reconstruction under Republican presidents Andrew Johnson and Ulysses S. Grant. For a brief period, Republicans assumed control of Southern politics, forcing drastic reforms and frequently giving former slaves positions in government. Reconstruction came to an end with the election of Rutherford B. Hayes through the Compromise of 1877.

Republicans benefitted from the Democrats' association with the Confederacy and dominated national politics.

Though states' rights was a cause of both Northern and Southern states before the War, control of the federal government led the Republican Party down a national line. The patriotric unity that developed in the North because of the War led to a string of military men as President, and an era of international expansion and domestic protectionism. As the rural Northern antebellum economy mushroomed with industry and immigration, supporting invention and business became the hallmarks of Republican policy proposals. From the Reconstruction era up to the turn of the century, the Republicans benefitted from the Democrats' association with the Confederacy and dominated national politics— albeit with strong competition from the Democrats during the 1880s especially. With the two-term presidency of Ulysses S. Grant, the party became known for its strong advocacy of commerce, industry, and veterans' rights, which continued through the end of the 19th century.

The progressive, protectionist, political, and beloved William McKinley was the last Civil War veteran elected President and embodied the Republican ideals of economic progress, invention, education, and patriotism. After McKinley's assassination, President Roosevelt tapped McKinley's Industrial Commission for his trust-busting ideas and continued the federal and nationalist policies of his predecessor.

Roosevelt decided not to run again in 1908 and chose William Howard Taft to replace him, but the widening division between progressive and conservative forces in the party resulted in a third-party candidacy for Roosevelt in the election of 1912. He beat Taft, but the split in the Republican vote resulted in a decisive victory for Democrat Woodrow Wilson, temporarily interrupting the Republican era.

Subsequent years saw the party firmly committed to laissez-faire economics, but the Great Depression cost it the presidency with the landslide election of Franklin Roosevelt in 1932. Roosevelt's New Deal Coalition controlled American politics for most of the next three decades, excepting the two-term presidency of war hero Dwight Eisenhower.

The Republican Party came to be split along new lines between a conservative wing (dominant in the West) and a liberal wing (dominant in New England)—combined with a residual base of inherited Midwestern Republicanism active throughout the century. The seeds of conservative dominance in the Republican Party were planted in the nomination of Barry Goldwater over Nelson Rockefeller as the Republican candidate for the 1964 presidential election. Goldwater represented the conservative wing of the party, while Rockefeller represented the liberal wing.

Goldwater's success in the deep south, and Nixon's successful Southern strategy four years later represented a significant political change, as Southern whites began moving into the party, largely due to Democrats' support for the Civil Rights Movement. Simultaneously, the remaining pockets of liberal Republicanism in the Northeast died out as the region turned solidly Democratic. In *The Emerging Republican Majority*, Kevin Phillips, then a Nixon strategist, argued (based on the 1968 election results) that support from Southern whites and growth in the Sun Belt, among other factors, was driving an enduring Republican realignment.

While his predictions were obviously somewhat overstated, the trends described could be seen in the Goldwater-inspired candidacy and 1980 election of Ronald Reagan and in the Gingrich-led "Republican Revolution" of 1994. The latter was the first time in 40 years that the Republicans secured control of both houses of Congress.

That year, the GOP campaigned on a platform of major reforms of government with measures, such as a balanced budget amendment to the Constitution and welfare reform. These measures and others formed the famous Contract with America, which was passed by Congress. Democratic President Bill Clinton stymied many of the initiatives contained therein, with welfare reform as a notable exception. In 1995, a budget battle with Clinton led to the brief shutdown of the federal government, an event which is often credited with assisting Clinton's victory in the 1996 election.

With the election of George W. Bush in 2000, the Republican party controlled both the presidency and both houses of Congress for the first time since 1952. Commentators speculate, and Republicans hope, that this may constitute a political realignment, catalyzed by decades of Cold War conflict and free market politics.

The Republican Party solidified its Congressional margins in the 2002 midterm elections, bucking the historic trend. It marked just the third time since the Civil War that the party in control of the White House gained seats in both houses of Congress in a midterm election (others were 1902 and 1934).

The Chieftains and the Church[2]

By TED HALSTEAD
ATLANTIC MONTHLY, JANUARY/FEBRUARY 2004

This year marks the 150th anniversary of the rivalry between the Democratic and Republican Parties. Ever since 1854, when the implosion of the Whigs paved the way for the birth of the Republican Party (26 years after the emergence of the Democrats), this rivalry has dominated and even defined American politics. Although the reign of these two parties has endured for well over half the life of our republic, it would be a mistake to assume that either party has remained consistent—or even recognizable.

Quick—which party stands for small government, states' rights, and laissez-faire economics? Which favors an activist federal government, public infrastructure projects, and expanded civil rights? Today the answers would be Republican and Democratic, respectively. Yet each party was founded on precisely the principles now associated with the other. And consider that the South, originally a stronghold of the Democrats, is now the anchor of the Republicans. But the most dramatic inversion in partisan identity is this: the Republicans in recent years have emerged as revolutionaries, while the Democrats have relegated themselves to defending tradition and the status quo.

The 150th anniversary of their rivalry provides an occasion for an intellectual audit of these two ever changing parties.

The Party of the Church

Let's begin with the Republicans, who under President George W. Bush have become the party of big ideas. There is no denying the range and boldness of their initiatives, from privatizing Social Security to institutionalizing a doctrine of preventive warfare; from eliminating taxes on capital gains and dividends to pulling out of numerous international treaties; from encouraging school choice to remaking the Middle East. This boldness is in itself an anomaly for a party that in past decades has tended to revere inherited norms and institutions, but it is just one of the signs that this is not the Republican Party of George W.'s father. Indeed, its identity seems to have no clear lineage.

The modern Republican tradition is usually thought to have originated with the firebrand rhetoric of Barry Goldwater, which ultimately paved the way for the two-term presidency of Ronald

---

2. Article by Ted Halstead from *Atlantic Monthly* January/February 2004. Copyright © Ted Halstead. Reprinted with permission.

Reagan. The Reagan revolution was built on three unifying princi-ples: anti-communism, social conservatism, and limited govern-ment. The sudden end of the Cold War left the Republicans with only two of these principles around which to organize. But most Americans let it be known that they were not particularly interested in fighting domestic culture wars, much less in turning back the clock on newfound personal freedoms. The Republican Party's anti-government agenda, meanwhile, culminated in the Gingrich revolu-tion of 1994, which sought to downsize all sorts of federal programs. To Newt Gingrich's surprise, the majority of Americans didn't really want a dramatic cutback in government programs and perceived his agenda as extremist.

George W. Bush is the first Republican President to recognize that the constituency for the Goldwater-Reagan-Gingrich anti-govern-ment crusade is dwindling—inspiring him to try to reposition his party. Although Bush calls his new and improved governing philoso-phy "compassionate conservatism," a more accurate description might be "big-spending conservatism."

Unlike Reagan, who shrank nondefense spending considerably and vetoed a number of spending bills in his first three years, Bush has so far increased total federal spending by a dizzying 20.4 per-cent and has yet to veto a single spending bill. The contrast is all the more dramatic when Bush is compared with Bill Clinton, who declared the end of big government, who in his first three years increased total government spending by only 3.5 percent, and who actually reduced discretionary spending by 8.8 percent. Clinton's Republican successor is quietly reversing course with a vengeance, leading the libertarian Cato Institute to accuse Bush of "governing like a Frenchman."

The President's reason for engineering this reversal, apparently, is to overcome the budgetary obstacles to parts of his agenda. For example, he seeks to privatize public services and enhance individ-ual choice—school choice, retirement choice (through private Social Security accounts), and medical choice (through private health insurance instead of government-run programs). But moving from one-size-fits-all government programs to more-flexible privatized ones may require more public outlay, not less, than simply preserv-ing the status quo. As the price for bringing competition into Medi-care, for instance, Bush enacted a prescription-drug benefit that represents the largest expansion in entitlements since Lyndon Johnson's Great Society. And moving to private Social Security accounts would entail funding two entirely separate systems during the transition period.

Fighting the war on terrorism, too, is expensive. But rather than adjusting his agenda accordingly, Bush has pushed through three huge tax cuts in as many years. In the process he has fatally under-mined the coherence of his overall program. Fusing vast new spending with deep tax cuts, Bush is locking into place long-term structural deficits whose costs to both our nation and the Republican Party would be difficult to overstate.

To understand why the Republican majority in Congress is playing along with the President, it helps to think of today's Republican Party as a theocracy; call it the Party of the Church. Under Bush the party is guided by a core ideology that it pursues with a near religious fervor, regardless of countervailing facts, changing circumstances, or even opposition among the conservative ranks. The President and his inner circle not only set the canon but demand—and usually get—strict compliance from Republican legislators in both houses of Congress. The two central tenets of Bush's orthodoxy are tax cuts and regime change in Iraq. He has staked the success of his presidency on them.

In the Party of the Church the theologians' role is played by hundreds of conservative scholars in think tanks, at publications, and on radio talk shows. That the academy is missing from this list is

> *In the Party of the Church the theologians'*
> *role is played by hundreds of conservative*
> *scholars in think tanks, at publications,*
> *and on radio talk shows.*

not an accident: conservative scholars could not find comfortable perches within university settings. But being banished from the academy served the Republican theologians remarkably well, because it enabled them to cultivate a style of argument and writing far better suited to reaching—and converting—both the public and politicians. The infrastructure of conservative thought is as well financed as it is complex; it includes seminaries in which to train conservative young scholars (the Heritage Foundation even has special dormitories for its interns), and what might be thought of as separate "orders," each upholding a slightly different school of thought—from the libertarians to the social conservatives to the neoconservatives. This sprawling idea machine produces not only policy innovations but also the language ("welfare queens," "the death tax") with which to sell the party's agenda.

Not surprisingly, the Party of the Church is highly moralistic. President Bush tends to frame issues in terms of ethical absolutes: good and evil, right and wrong. Moralism may or may not make for good politics, but it rarely makes for good policy, because it substitutes wishful and parochial thinking for careful analysis. Its ascendancy reflects a broader shift in the Republican Party—a shift away from an identity that was secular, pragmatic, and northeastern toward one that, like the President himself, is more evangelical and southern. Nowhere is this more evident than in foreign policy, where Bush—reviving what the historian Walter Russell Mead calls the Jacksonian tradition—is turning his back on both the real-politik of Richard Nixon and the conservative internationalism of Reagan and his own father, making pre-emption rather than containment the central organizing principle and favoring unilateral action over multilateral diplomacy. In doing so Bush has discarded hundreds of years of international law and decades of American tradition. The most immediate cost is that the United States has alienated much of the world in the name of making it safe.

"Supply-side Keynesianism"

When it comes to economic orthodoxy, the Party of the Church is no more consistent with traditional Republican principles. Although the Republicans claim to be devoted to free markets, most of the big economic interests identified with the party are surprisingly dependent on federal subsidies, protectionism, or both. The most obvious examples are southern growers of cotton, sugar, oranges, and peanuts, and midwestern producers of grain. The Administration is so committed to shielding these interests from global competition that it elected to let the Cancún round of trade negotiations collapse—dealing a significant blow to the prospects for expanded free trade—rather than pressure Congress to reduce U.S. agricultural subsidies. In similar fashion, the Bush Administration supports lavish federal subsidies for a wide range of extractive industries (including oil, gas, and coal) and for cattle ranching.

No assessment of the modern Republican Party would be complete without a discussion of the elaborate mythology of supply-side economics, whose logic has been strained to the breaking point under Bush's watch. The basic supply-side argument is that tax cuts increase the incentive to work, save, and invest, which boosts economic growth. During the Reagan years such logic was used to argue that slashing tax rates would actually increase tax revenues, by producing additional growth—but this has long since been dismissed by mainstream economists and shown false by the record of history. The party also uses supply-side economics to justify tax cuts that are disproportionately skewed in favor of the well-to-do, on the grounds that they are the most likely to save and invest. This argument has always been suspect, and it is even less credible in the aftermath of the technology bubble; the economic woes of the past few years have been due not to lack of investment but, rather, to an excess of capacity.

By sticking with the old supply-side formula—cut taxes as often as possible, especially for the wealthy—Bush has delivered a particularly costly and inefficient stimulus package to help the nation out of its economic downturn. And the Administration seems to recognize as much, given that it has hedged its bets by marrying large supply-side tax cuts with equally large demand-side spending increases, yielding an odd hybrid that might be called "supply-side Keynesianism." This contradictory policy suggests that not even

Republicans still believe in the magic of their standard fix. Yet they are not about to abandon the myth. It is far too sacrosanct and convenient an article of faith in the Republican canon.

A major risk in combining moralism and policy, evidently, is that dogma often trumps intellectual honesty. This is particularly clear in the case of official claims that the Administration's overall economic agenda is aimed at helping middle-class families. A more candid articulation of its domestic-policy vision appeared in a June 2003 *Washington Post* op-ed article by Grover Norquist, one of the most influential of conservative strategists. "The new Republican policy is an annual tax cut," Norquist wrote; he predicted that Bush would proceed step by step to abolish estate and capital-gains taxes altogether, to exempt all savings from taxation, and to move the nation to a flat tax on wages only. Implicit in this vision is not only a grand contradiction—cutting taxes while raising spending is unsustainable—but also a significant shift in the burden of taxation from the wealthy to the working class and the poor. Apparently the contemporary Republican Party does remain faithful to at least one old conservative belief, which Clinton Rossiter, in his book *Conservatism in America*, described nearly 50 years ago as "the inevitability and necessity of social classes."

> *If the Republicans are now the Party of the Church, then the Democrats are the Party of the Chieftains.*

The Party of the Chieftains

For its part, the Democratic Party suffers from a different sort of incoherence: plagued by constant squabbling among the interest groups that make up its base, it cannot agree on a clear message or purpose. The sheer breadth of the Democratic coalition is remarkable: it includes organized labor, teachers' and other public employees' unions, environmentalists, racial minorities (especially African-Americans), Hollywood, trial lawyers, the gray lobby, the gay lobby, civil libertarians, pro-choice activists, and a good bit of Wall Street. Although this breadth might seem to be an asset for the Democrats, all these groups are veto-wielding factions when it comes to their respective chunks of the policy turf. This can be downright paralyzing.

If the Republicans are now the Party of the Church, then the Democrats are the Party of the Chieftains. They treat an election almost like a parade: groups that otherwise have little in common come together every year or two, only to return to their niches afterward. The multiplicity of purpose is all the more evident when the party is out of office. During his eight-year presidency Clinton relied on his political skill and charisma—and the benefits of a growing economy—to keep most Democratic factions happy and essentially reading from the same playbook.

When Bush took office, however, the deep tensions among the Democrats resurfaced. For instance, take the relationship between Wall Street and Main Street. Under the New Deal, when U.S. industry was little challenged by competition from abroad, workers and owners of capital managed to reach common ground on a number of issues, from workers' rights to basic benefits. But the subsequent globalization of manufacturing and services led to the collapse of this alliance. Thus whereas Wall Street and some high-tech firms favor financial liberalization, copyright protection, balanced budgets, and a strong dollar (to make imported goods less expensive), working-class Americans want curbs on job flight, tougher international labor standards, strengthened safety nets, and a weaker dollar (to boost exports of the goods they manufacture). The fiercer the global competition, the fiercer the tension between these traditional Democratic camps. The party is just as torn on social issues: Hollywood, members of minorities, and civil libertarians favor identity politics, social liberalism, and political correctness, whereas this agenda tends to offend the sensibilities of working-class white men.

In the run-up to this year's primaries, the tensions among the Democratic Chieftains have culminated in an all-out struggle for their party's soul, with one camp claiming to represent the "Democratic wing" and another claiming to represent the "electable wing." Although the feuding is over style as well as substance, at least three issues clearly divide left and center: the left is resolutely against the war in Iraq, whereas the center defends it (though averring that it should have been conducted in a more multilateral fashion); the left wants to repeal all Bush's tax cuts, whereas the center favors repealing only some; and the left is wary of unregulated free trade, whereas the center embraces free trade and globalization. In many ways this is a battle over the Clinton legacy. Clintonian centrists fear that the party's new image on welfare, crime, free trade, foreign policy, and fiscal policy—which they worked so hard to establish—will be undermined by a nominee from the party's left.

Fiscal responsibility is another major source of tension within the Democratic Party. Ever since Clinton salvaged the party's credibility in this area, Democrats have tried to build on that new reputation. But those efforts produced two serious problems for the party, one short-term and one longer-term. Over the past three years, while the economy was weak, it may have been a mistake for the Democrats to hew to a policy of fiscal rectitude—especially when it prevented them from thinking creatively about a temporary stimulus package. Maintaining fiscal discipline over the longer term, however, is truly important. Yet it is unclear whether the Democrats will be able to do so given all the programs the various Chieftains are demanding. The race for the Democratic presidential nomination has thrown this conflict into sharp relief. All the contenders cite fiscal prudence as grounds for repealing some or all of Bush's tax cuts—but all then propose to spend the money thus recouped on everything from expanding health insurance to improving schools. From a budgetary perspective there is no difference between decreasing public revenue through tax cuts and increasing public spending through new programs. The Democrats could argue that theirs is a more compassionate form of fiscal irresponsibility (it's better to have health insurance for children than tax cuts for the rich), but they can't argue that they're being any more fiscally responsible than George Bush.

Regardless of who emerges as the Democratic nominee or which camp he hails from, the bulk of his agenda may be disturbingly predictable and backward-looking. Given the power of the Chieftains, it is almost a certainty that the Democratic candidate in 2004 will be against school choice (to appease teachers' unions) and Social Security reform (the gray lobby), and in favor of affirmative action (minorities) and employer-based health care (organized labor). In these and other ways he will be a defender of the status quo. As Al Sharpton recently put it, approvingly, the Democrats are now the true conservatives.

Trapped in the Past

In its legitimate desire to preserve the achievements of the New Deal and the Great Society, the Democratic Party has become trapped in the past, routinely defending antiquated industrial-era programs even when these no longer serve their original ends. George Santayana once defined fanaticism as redoubling your efforts when you have forgotten your aim. Democrats are no fanatics, but they are increasingly guilty of confusing ends and means. Consider employer-based health insurance. The link between health insurance and employment was an accident of history, devised in a bygone era when spending one's working lifetime with a single company was the norm. Now that most Americans change employers every couple of years, does it make sense to rely on a system that forces one to change insurers—or, worse, risk losing coverage—every time? And when it comes to protecting Social Security, the Democrats are waging a battle against immutable demographic forces: a program that originated when working-age Americans far outnumbered retirees cannot remain essentially unchanged in a rapidly aging society.

Underlying this abdication of new thinking is a still more troubling liability: the Party of the Chieftains does not trust the American people to make responsible choices for themselves. Although the Democrats are known as the "pro-choice" party, the kinds of choice they are most eager to defend are in the private realm—reproduction and lifestyle. When it comes to the public sphere

The Party of the Chieftains does not trust the American people to make responsible choices for themselves.

(where your child goes to school, or how to invest your Social Security contributions), the Democrats tend to oppose expanding individual choice, largely because some of the leading Chieftains fear that it would weaken their own influence. The Chieftains' reluctance also derives in part from a fear that public programs with more options would undermine equity; but it's possible to devise creative new programs to enhance flexibility and fairness at the same time. Regardless of their reasons, in resisting the expansion of individual choice, a sine qua non of any successful information-age politics, the Democrats have positioned themselves on the wrong side of history.

This inability to advance creative policy solutions hints at yet another problem for the Democrats; the Party of the Chieftains is so busy playing defense that it has forgotten how to play offense. When the Republicans were in the minority during the early Clinton years, they introduced one bold proposal after another—never expecting that these would pass in the short run, but hoping to galvanize the party and set precedents for the future. To a considerable degree this worked. In contrast, the Democrats have spent the past three years turning timidity into an art form, allowing President Bush to set the terms of the debate and confining themselves to criticizing his agenda rather than venturing one of their own. This is the case even in the foreign-policy arena: other than vague calls for multilateralism and diplomacy, it's unclear how a Democratic grand strategy would differ from the President's.

In short, the Democrats have failed utterly to replenish the intellectual capital on which any party's success ultimately hinges. Whereas the Republicans can turn to large, multi-issue think tanks for guidance and inspiration, the Democrats have mainly single-issue groups—environmentalists, civil-rights activists, women's-rights activists—with neither the capacity nor the incentive to forge a greater whole. The flimsiness and Balkanization of the Democratic intellectual infrastructure owes much to the proclivities of progressive philanthropies, which are far more likely to invest in grassroots demonstration programs than in the war of ideas, and which tend to award grants that are strictly limited to particular subject areas, thereby discouraging cross-pollination. Lacking other options, most liberal scholars therefore gravitate to the academy—which actually inhibits them from shaping the public debate. As academic disciplines become ever more specialized, professors are encouraged to publish in esoteric journals—whose only audience is other professors—rather than in the popular press. Whereas conservative scholars have influence far out of proportion to their numbers, liberal scholars have numbers far out of proportion to their influence.

Not only is the Party of the Chieftains at a loss for new ideas, but it lacks a language for defending its core values. In part this is because the Chieftains like to describe their respective constituencies as victims in order to secure concessions from a party that tends to root for the underdog. Republicans, in contrast, are likely to address citizens as if they were all just around the corner from becoming millionaires. This creates a perception that the Republicans are the party of winners and the Democrats the party of losers.

During the Great Depression, when it was painfully obvious that citizens were vulnerable to forces beyond their control, it was easier for a Democratic leader such as FDR to craft a message of collective well-being—that all Americans would be better off if each American were given a helping hand by the government. Nowadays American culture increasingly emphasizes the opposite message: that individuals are to blame for their own problems. Yet the profound dislocations caused by globalization and technological change make the need for an overarching vision of a better society just as urgent as it was in FDR's time.

"The success of a party," Woodrow Wilson claimed, "means little except when the nation is using that party for a large and definite purpose." By this standard both the Party of the Church and the Party of the Chieftains are failures. The Republicans are handicapped by an ideology holding that it is somehow possible to pursue big-spending conservatism at home and an interventionist military program abroad while cutting taxes repeatedly. The Democrats, meanwhile, are paralyzed by the micro-agendas of numerous feuding factions. Both parties wear straitjackets of their own design.

The American people deserve better—and they know it, to judge by the legions of self-described "independents." Fortunately, our major parties are mere vessels; the principles, agendas, and coalitions they contain can vary dramatically from decade to decade. It is just a matter of time, history suggests, until both parties are reinvented. Let us hope they will improve.

Election Is Turning Novices Into Political Advocates[3]

By Elisabeth Rosenthal
The New York Times, April 3, 2004

For 20 years, Al Puchala was in political hibernation. So was his sometime investment partner, Douglas Korn. They were busy with other things: career, marriage, children, charities. Sure, they voted as a civic duty, but in their world of high finance, politics was considered a private thing—rude if openly displayed.

But this is 2004. People are mad. The world is scary. So here come two high-powered executives who are friends and associates, jumping into the trenches of American presidential politics on opposite sides.

Mr. Puchala, a private equity fund manager, is vetting position papers for the Democratic National Committee and setting up an issues bank to help Democratic candidates. He is writing checks. He is roping in musician friends to set up benefit concerts.

On a recent Thursday night his stately white colonial here [Westport, Connecticut] was used for a get-together and fund-raiser for Diane Farrell, a Democratic Congressional candidate. The house, decked out in red, white, and blue balloons, overflowed with people like him—casually dressed, 40-something political first-timers.

Mr. Korn helped organize a reception for President Bush in nearby Greenwich. He is soliciting donations like crazy, raising more than $100,000 and thereby rising to the rank of "Pioneer." A shelf in his office at Bear Stearns sports newly framed photographs showing him with the president and Vice President Dick Cheney.

Both men say the political bug bit them this year because they sensed a new urgency in the post-9/11 world. In 2000, they thought the choice of Bush vs. Gore did not matter. Today, they speak in apocalyptic language of historical turning points, of the desperate need to make the right choice.

Mr. Puchala: "We feel like this administration is really leading the country in the wrong direction. To a fiscal disaster. A foreign policy disaster. And it's kind of our turn to get involved and make a difference. The stakes are really high."

Mr. Korn: "If there ever was a time to get involved it is now, since I think the next five years will be a crucial point in modern history, related to the spread of weapons of mass destruction amidst the dangerous politics of radicalism in the Middle East. And I really

---

believe this administration has the right approach in terms of actively intervening in problems that are easier to ignore. To my mind, if we revert back to failed policies of the past, heaven help us all."

The two men, who remain friendly, are demographically indistinguishable: Ivy League–educated M.B.A.'s in their early 40's with offices in New York and homes and young families in suburban Connecticut. Political moderates, they mostly agree on social issues like welfare and women's rights.

But in this red-and-blue America, they find themselves staring across an ideological Grand Canyon. And they are not alone. After years in the doldrums, membership in local Democratic and Republican clubs has skyrocketed this year, the two parties say. Polls show that voter interest in the presidential race is 20 percent higher than it was at this time in the 2000 campaign.

"I haven't seen this kind of passion and activism in this country since 1968 or '72," said Ken Sherrill, a political scientist at Hunter

---

"You get to a stage in life where you realize that it's not just about you but about your country, your community and the world."—
Douglas Korn, George W. Bush fund-raiser

College in New York. "The sheer intensity of the anger is really extraordinary, the kind of thing you usually associate with the religious right."

Last time, Mr. Puchala voted for Al Gore and Mr. Korn voted for George W. Bush, but who really cared? "People felt really disenfranchised and had kind of given up on the system," Mr. Puchala said. "Now we've gone through four years of war, 9/11, from surplus to deficit. No one can be complacent."

Like many of their successful contemporaries, Mr. Puchala and Mr. Korn went straight from college to law or business school, then dived headlong into remunerative careers. Now they are taking stock.

"You get to a stage in life where you realize that it's not just about you but about your country, your community and the world," Mr. Korn said. "One day you realize that you have the ability to make a meaningful contribution and shame on you if you don't."

The shift is striking in the world of high finance, where politics, once considered bad for business, is now the center of office conversations. Mr. Korn grins and explains that he displays his photos of Republican officials in part to tease the many Democrats in his office.

Mr. Puchala has drawn all his closest friends in Westport into action, tapping in to their various skills. Crispin Cioe, a composer and musician, is organizing a benefit concert for the Democratic

Party. Andy Moss, a technology executive and former independent who says he "could have voted either way in the 2000 election," is advising the party on science issues.

Arlo Ellison switched his affiliation to Democrat from Republican just three months ago, dismayed by the Republican record on deficit spending.

"It is a huge move for me to be an active Democrat," Mr. Ellison said in a phone interview. "But as a political rookie, I'll do anything to help out."

At his Harvard Business School reunion last fall, Mr. Korn and his old friend Howard Morgan suddenly found themselves talking politics and discovered they were both enthusiastic Republicans.

"Normally, polite people in our work didn't talk much about politics, but this has been a great opportunity to meet like-minded people," Mr. Morgan recalled. "We both said, 'Boy, we wish we could get more involved,' and we've since been sort of mutually supportive in navigating the system."

In January, Mr. Korn and Mr. Morgan were hosts for a huge benefit for President Bush in Greenwich.

On both sides of the fence, there is a snowball effect, as friend infects friend with the political bug.

The two camps have viewed the events of the last four years through very different lenses and hold their political beliefs with the passion of converts.

Those who tend Republican see attacks on the United States as evidence that American values are under a serious threat that demands aggressive action.

Democrats, in contrast, are convinced that the Bush administration's response to terrorism has been intemperate, and say that has made the world dangerous. They also criticize the Republicans as hypocrites for deficit spending.

The rancor is also partly a result of the 2000 election.

"Democrats sit on a high horse and want to say that Bush was not popularly elected," Mr. Morgan said. "I'd love to knock that down."

Many Democrats, meanwhile, have lingering suspicions that treachery and big money stole that election, and are vowing it will never happen again.

Mr. Moss, the technology executive, could have been speaking for the newly energized of both parties when he said: "There are a lot of people like me who grew up just after the '60s, so remember it but weren't part of the process. Somewhere along the way we got detached from the politics. But at some point you wake up and realize that the adults won't do it for you—that you are the adults. And you can't just sit on the sidelines and comment."

Third-party Candidates Make Issues Resonate[4]

By Jim Eskin
San Antonio Business Journal, March 19, 2004

Ralph Nader continues the longstanding tradition of third-party candidates who have spanned the breadth of the ideological spectrum and been some of our most colorful political figures. He is also fighting the odds. Since 1852, every U.S. president has been either a Republican or a Democrat.

Ours is commonly called a "two-party system" because there have historically been only two major political parties with candidates competing for offices (especially in federal elections).

This is the result of the way U.S. elections are structured. Representatives in the Congress and in state legislatures are elected in single-member districts where the individual with the most votes wins. Since only one party's candidate can win in each district, there is a strong incentive for political competitors to organize themselves into two opposing sides. By doing so, party members and their candidates maximize their chances of winning.

In countries where there are multi-member districts, parties that win smaller percentages of the vote can often secure legislative representation. In these systems, there is an incentive to form smaller third parties. Other features of our elections, such as campaign finance rules, the Electoral College, and rules giving party candidates ballot access further solidify the two-party system.

So are third parties good or bad for our democracy?

This much is clear: they wreak havoc on a political system built on the structure and stability of two-party contests. Candidates with strong regional appeal like George Wallace, who won 46 southern electors in 1968, can throw an election into the House of Representatives, which brings along all sorts of bizarre consequences. Even if they don't pick up electoral votes and garner small percentages of votes in critical states, they can be spoilers and determine the occupant in the White House.

As the Green Party's nominee in 2000, Nader appeared on the ballot in 43 states and the District of Columbia. In Florida and New Hampshire, President Bush won such narrow victories that had Gore received the bulk of Nader's votes in those states, he would have been elected.

---

4. Article by Jim Eskin from *San Antonio Business Journal*, March 19, 2004. Copyright © 2004 *San Antonio Business Journal*. Reprinted with permission of the publisher.

On the policy side, third parties have played a positive role as champions of sweeping reforms. The Socialist Party promoted women's suffrage for many years culminating in the ratification of the 19th Amendment in 1920, and first advocated laws establishing minimum ages and limiting hours of work for children that culminated in the Keating-Owen Act in 1916. Thank the Populist Party for the 40-hour workweek. Their support for reduced working hours starting in the 19th century led to the Fair Labor Standards Act of 1938.

Typically, as third parties begin to resonate with voters, their successes are short-lived. In most cases, their issues or ideas are usurped by candidates of the two major parties. Sometimes their issue positions are even incorporated into the platforms of dominant parties. With no unique issues to stand on and depleted voter support, third parties generally fade away.

While there are a number of third parties in the U.S.—from the American Communist Party on the far left to numerous parties in the center and the far right—only a few have wielded significant political influence. Still third-party presidential candidates have had their moments. The highest total was achieved by Teddy Roosevelt in 1912, who posted 27.5 percent of the vote, followed by Millard Fillmore in 1856 with 21.5 percent, and Ross Perot in 1992 with 18.9 percent.

In American political history, third parties have by and large served the important purpose of focusing the two major political parties on issues they have ignored or dealt with ineffectively. Don't expect a third party to emerge as one of the major parties by knocking an existing one off its roost. Don't expect one of their candidates to win. But do expect them to play a real role shaping and influencing the issues and debates of the day.

Third-party and Independent Candidates

The United States is often thought of as a two-party system. In practical effect it is: either a Democrat or a Republican has occupied the White House every year since 1852. At the same time, however, the country has produced a plethora of third and minor parties over the years. For example, 58 parties were represented on at least one state ballot during the 1992 presidential elections. Among these were such obscure parties as the Apathy, the Looking Back, the New Mexico Prohibition, the Tish Independent Citizens and the Vermont Taxpayers.

In general, third parties organize around a single issue or set of issues. They tend to fare best when they have a charismatic leader. With the presidency out of reach, most seek a platform to publicize their political and social concerns.

Theodore Roosevelt. The most successful third party candidate of this century was a Republican, Theodore Roosevelt, the former president. His Progressive or Bull Moose Party won 27.4 percent of the vote in the 1912 election. The progressive wing of the Republican Party, having grown disenchanted with President William Howard Taft, whom Roosevelt had hand-picked as his successor, urged Roosevelt to seek the party nomination in 1912. This he did, defeating Taft in a number of primaries. Taft controlled the party machinery, however, and secured the nomination.

Roosevelt's supporters then broke away and formed the Progressive Party. Declaring himself as fit as a bull moose (hence the party's popular name), Roosevelt campaigned on a platform of regulating "big business," women's suffrage, a graduated income tax, the Panama Canal, and conservation. His effort was sufficient to defeat Taft. By splitting the Republican vote, however, he helped ensure the election of the Democrat Woodrow Wilson.

Socialists. The Socialist Party also reached its high point in 1912, attaining 6 percent of the popular vote. Perennial candidate Eugene Debs won over 900,000 votes that year, advocating collective ownership of the transportation and communication industries, shorter working hours, and public works projects to spur employment. Jailed for sedition during World War I, Debs campaigned from his cell in 1920, but neither he nor his successors ever duplicated the results of 1912.

Robert LaFollette. Another Progressive was Senator Robert LaFollette, who won 16.6 percent of the vote in the 1924 election. Long a champion of farmers and industrial workers, and an ardent foe of big business, LaFollette was a prime mover in the recreation of the Progressive movement following World War I. Backed by the farm and labor vote, as well as by Socialists and remnants of Roosevelt's Bull Moose Party, LaFollette ran on a platform of nationalizing railroads and the country's natural resources. He also strongly supported increased taxation on the wealthy and the right of collective bargaining. Despite a strong showing in certain regions, he carried only his home state of Wisconsin.

Henry Wallace. The Progressive Party reinvented itself in 1948 with the nomination of Henry Wallace, a former secretary of agriculture and vice president under Franklin Roosevelt. Briefly Harry Truman's secretary of commerce, he was fired for opposing Truman's firm stand against the Soviet Union. Wallace's 1948 platform opposed the Cold War, the Marshall Plan, and big business. He also campaigned to end discrimination against blacks and women, backed a minimum wage, and called for the elimination of the House Committee on Un-American Activities. His failure to repudiate the U.S. Communist Party, which had endorsed him, undermined his popularity and he wound up with just over 2.4 percent of the popular vote.

Dixiecrats. The same percentage was attained by the States Rights or Dixiecrat Party, led by South Carolina governor Strom Thurmond. Like the Progressives, the Dixiecrats broke away from the Democrats in 1948. Their opposition, however, stemmed not from Truman's Cold War policies, but his civil rights platform. Although defined in terms of "states rights," the party's main goal was continuing racial segregation and the "Jim Crow" laws which sustained it.

George Wallace. The racial and social upheavals of the 1960s helped bring George Wallace, another segregationist Southern governor, to national attention. Wallace built a following through his colorful attacks against civil rights, liberals, and the federal government. Founding the American Independent Party in 1968, he ran his campaign from the statehouse in Montgomery, Alabama, winning 13.5 percent of the overall presidential vote.

H. Ross Perot. Every third party seeks to capitalize on popular dissatisfaction with the major parties and the federal government. At few times in recent history, however, has this sentiment been as strong as it was during the 1992 election. A hugely wealthy Texas businessman, Perot possessed a knack for getting his message of economic common sense and fiscal responsibility across to a wide spectrum of American people.

Lampooning the nation's leaders and reducing his economic message to easily understood formulae, Perot found little difficulty gaining media attention. His campaign organization, United We Stand, was staffed primarily by volunteers and backed by his personal fortune. Far from resenting his wealth, many admired Perot's business success and the freedom it brought him from soliciting campaign funds from special interests.

Perot withdrew from the race in July. Re-entering it a month before the election, he won over 19 million votes, by far the largest number ever tallied by a third party candidate and second only to Roosevelt's 1912 showing as a percentage of the total.

Source: *usinfo.state.gov*

It's Not Your Father's Reform Party Anymore[5]

BY BREE HOCKING
ROLL CALL, APRIL 8, 2004

The 21st century has not been good to the Reform Party.

After bursting onto the national scene in the waning days of the past millennium as an alternative for those disillusioned with two-party politics—attracting millions of votes with Texas billionaire Ross Perot as its presidential candidate, electing a governor in Minnesota and securing recognition as a political party in 35 states—the party has foundered. It is racked by internal disputes and splinter groups and, in some cases, has seen even contested state chairmanships.

"There's no more party to belong to," said Russell Verney, the founding chairman of the Reform Party, who is now a self-described Independent. "Essentially, it has evaporated, it has gone away."

Today, the Reform Party boasts ballot access in only seven states, has just $2,000 in its coffers and is affiliated with roughly 20 state organizations, mainly "tiny little groups that aren't doing anything," said Richard Winger, editor of *Ballot Access News*, which tracks developments in third parties.

After seeing its presidential numbers decline from 8.4 percent of the vote in 1996 to just .5 percent (with two candidates running) in 2000, its 2003 convention attracted a mere 50 delegates.

What's more, according to Chairman Shawn O'Hara, the Federal Election Commission has determined that the party owes about $334,000 in misspent convention funds, a judgment the party is contesting in federal court.

In the eyes of many past and current Reform members, one man is to blame for the current malaise: Pat Buchanan, the Reform presidential candidate in 2000. His nomination precipitated a split within the party at the convention that summer in Long Beach, Calif., with one faction selecting Natural Law Party candidate John Hagelin as its nominee at a separate gathering.

"What Buchanan did was he went into states that already had parties formed and literally took over the states," said Ohio Reform Party Chairwoman Virginia Brooks. He "strong-armed the other people out."

The widespread confusion over who was the party's true nominee led at least one state—Connecticut—to leave both men off the ballot.

In the wake of the split, several leaders of the Buchanan faction regrouped in 2002 under the mantle of the America First Party, which has championed a socially conservative, economically populist platform. Some states, however, such as Michigan, have seen dueling Reform parties briefly emerge; in others, such as West Virginia, pro-Buchanan forces separated from the Reform Party USA, claiming its leadership was "illegal" and vowing to form a new national Reform Party.

Perot first ran on the Reform Party ticket in 1996—which grew out of his 1992 "United We Stand" political movement and independent presidential candidacy—though the party did not gain official national status until 1998, the year former wrestler Jesse Ventura was elected governor of Minnesota.

But from its earliest days, the Reform Party has had a conflicted history, with internal dissension often linked to Perot's position in

---

"It really turned out to be a cult of personality instead of a legitimate independent party."—Thomas D'Amore Jr., political consultant

---

the party, though according to Perot associate Verney, the Texan mogul played no official role in the party post-1997.

After the 1996 election, an initial fissure occurred when a group—primarily comprising supporters of former Colorado Gov. Dick Lamm (D), who had challenged Perot for the 1996 Reform presidential nomination—parted ways with the national party and formed the American Reform Party.

"It really turned out to be a cult of personality instead of a legitimate independent party," said political consultant Thomas D'Amore Jr., who ran Lamm's campaign and said Perot's commandeering of the 1996 election process "was the most undemocratic form of politics I've ever been involved with."

In early 2000, Ventura, the highest profile elected official, left the party over disputes with Perot allies and over the emergence of Buchanan as a major player in the party. After his departure, the Reform Party of Minnesota's name was changed back to the Independence Party of Minnesota, its original appellation.

Perot "was controlling everything from behind the scenes," charged former Sen. Dean Barkley (I-Minn.), a former Reform member and Ventura ally.

According to O'Hara, the party is in the process of reaffiliating several state organizations and believes its days of internal bickering are over.

"This is a Reform Party reaching people from all walks of life now," said O'Hara. "This isn't a Reform Party of the past."

In 2002, the party—which says Perot signed an affidavit in September 2000 certifying it as the national Reform Party deserving of any matching funds—rewrote much of the Buchanan-inspired conservative platform, though it remains staunchly opposed to free trade and illegal immigration. Late last year, the party moved its headquarters from Dallas—Perot's home turf—to Hattiesburg, Miss., where O'Hara lives.

A self-described "very happy millionaire," O'Hara made his fortune in real estate and is something of a political and intellectual dabbler. Over the years, he has launched numerous bids, on a variety of tickets, for both the U.S. Senate and the Mississippi governor's mansion—sometimes in races against his own father. He is running for the House this year in the district held by Rep. Bennie Thompson (D-Miss.).

The 46-year-old polymath—who says he is two courses away from attaining his sixth degree, a master's in business administration—has written and self-published no less than 1,112 books, with the aim of securing a spot in the *Guinness Book of World Records*. He once filled a 14-foot U-Haul truck with the volumes and presented them to a local elementary school for inspection. In his spare time, he has also penned 120 movie screenplays, 33 musicals, and 3,600 songs.

It is not surprising that under O'Hara's leadership, the party, which will likely run only four nonpresidential federal candidates this cycle, has branched out into some less than conventional realms.

O'Hara used October's national convention in Diamondhead, Miss., to showcase his self-produced film "Rebel Lady," a romantic comedy about a stripper out for vengeance after being unjustly incarcerated in a mental institution. The film featured 10 Reform Party candidates, with O'Hara himself in a lead role. (O'Hara later married his co-star, Amanda Rios, 21, and says he plans to enter the picture in the Sundance film festival.)

But the style and focus of the national party has done little to endear it to some of its state organizations.

In November, the Michigan Reform Party—not to be confused with the Reform Party of Michigan, from which the group split over disagreements as to who was the legitimate chairman—registered with the FEC as the Independence Party of Michigan because of what it viewed as a widespread lack of focus in the national party. It is now working in a loose coalition with the Reform parties of Texas and Florida, as well as with the Independence Party of Delaware with the intent of eventually bringing the groups together on a national level as the Independence Party USA, said Matt Johnson, the party's 21-year-old chairman.

"The Reform Party USA is in such a weakened state, we feel we probably have more members in our state party than in the entire Reform Party USA put together," he said.

The Michigan party's move comes on the heels of numerous other disaffiliations, which have occurred since the divisive 2000 convention, most notably the departure of the Independence parties of Minnesota and New York, once two of the Reform Party's most active state organizations.

And as one-time candidates such as Smithereens lead singer Pat DiNizio discovered, some state Reform parties never rose to the level required of an effective political machine.

"There was no organization, no support," said former Reform Party New Jersey Senatorial contender DiNizio, who lost to now-Sen. Jon Corzine (D) in 2000. "When I met some of the people who were in charge of the New Jersey faction of the Reform Party, they didn't know who I was, and I was their candidate."

Still, despite its detractors and weak national position, the party is pushing ahead. O'Hara met last week with former Green Party presidential candidate Ralph Nader in Georgia to discuss the possibility of Nader running on the Reform ticket this year, with Nader's decision expected as early as today, said O'Hara. The party's convention will be held July 22–25 at the University Plaza Hotel and Convention Center in Columbus, Ohio, with Hutton Gibson (Mel Gibson's father) as a possible keynote speaker.

And for the relentlessly optimistic Reform faithful, the horizon still holds the possibility of a brighter electoral future.

"Ross Perot left us with one great legacy—the party itself," said Brooks, the Ohio chairwoman. "I truly believe the third-party movement is going to take hold, and it's going to go like wild fire."

III. The Nominating Process: From Caucus to Convention

Editor's Introduction

T he processes by which political parties select their presidential nominees have changed dramatically over the years. The first nominating convention was held in the 1820s by the long-defunct Anti-Masonic party, and the Whigs and Democrats soon began to hold conventions themselves. For the next 150 years or so, presidential nominees were chosen at conventions. Delegates representing all the states would congregate in a particular city in order to reach a consensus on a nominee. The convention was a time for speeches, demonstrations of party unity, and backroom meetings by insiders as they sought to nominate a candidate palatable to all. At times conventions could become violent affairs with physical fights on the floor and confrontations outside between police and demonstrators.

During the second half of the 20th century, the convention began to be supplanted in the nominating process by primaries and caucuses. In a primary the members of a particular party in a specific state head to the polls to register their choice for the nomination. Whoever wins a state receives an allotment of that state's delegates; currently, in Republican primaries, the winner is awarded all of a state's delegates, while in Democratic primaries the delegates received are in proportion to a candidate's total percentage of the vote. The emergence of the primary system resulted from a variety of factors: First, the primary was perceived as more democratic than a convention, as it allowed all voters who were party members, not just an elite group of delegates and insiders, to play a role in the selection process. Second, the emergence of television and the visual media drastically altered the dynamics of political campaigning: A candidate's ability to connect with voters, rather than just party bigwigs, became increasingly important, and the primary election proved an important bellwether of a potential nominee's hold on the electorate; moreover, television coverage of the at times chaotic and divisive political conventions, particularly the 1968 Democratic convention in Chicago, served to tarnish the eventual nominee in the general election. In response the parties sought to eliminate any chance of chaos that could potentially hurt the party and the nominee. Thus, today, while political conventions are still held, they are bereft of any actual drama: That is, the nominee is already known to all, and his or her acceptance of the party's backing is a mere formality. The convention is used as a highly choreographed showcase of party unity geared exclusively toward attracting voters, rather than choosing a nominee.

Momentum is exceedingly important for a candidate in the party primaries. One victory can lead to another, and a front-runner generally has an easier time raising money to continue the campaign. Consequently, the two earliest contests, in Iowa and New Hampshire, have achieved greater and greater importance. In this section Alicia P. Stern offers detailed history of the Iowa caucus for the *Washington Times*, while Jack Spillane discusses the New Hampshire primary, the first primary in the nation. Chris Nammour, for PBS Online, describes the primary process more generally, noting certain days—like Super Tuesday—when a number of state contests are held. An excerpt from *Congressional Digest* provides an overview of the history and changing role of the party convention.

A Historic Perspective on Iowa Caucuses[1]

BY ALICIA P. STERN
THE WASHINGTON TIMES, JANUARY 16, 2004

It's a quadrennial rite of winter and it makes one of the smallest states in the nation one of the most attention-grabbing—at least for a week—but the results could reverberate through the White House for the next four years.

Iowa, a state of less than 3 million people, plays a key role for both Democratic and Republican parties in their presidential nomination process. The decisions made by gatherings of a few dozens Iowans often change the political options that larger parts of the country are left with.

Because of this, Iowa is something of a Mecca—presidential hopefuls must travel to the Heartland to prove worthy of their aspirations. In the summer prior to the Iowa caucuses, candidates descend on the Iowa State Fair, the annual showcase—2004 marks the 150th anniversary of the event—that draws hundreds of thousands of people to Des Moines.

From that time, candidates attend community functions in the parades, coffee shops, and meeting halls of small towns.

During this time national and international attention often focuses on Iowa, which certainly pleases the chambers of commerce across the state but the spotlight often quickly is pointed elsewhere, causing many locals to see the focus of the politicians and the media as fickle.

"I've heard people grumble about that over the years," Jack Lufkin, a curator at the Iowa Historical Building, told *United Press International*. "A lot of people say how much they care about Iowa and then, after the caucuses, you hardly ever see them again."

Lufkin cited Iowa farmers, who complain of a lack of political support once the campaigns are over.

Yet Lufkin himself seemed to have tremendous respect for the candidates and how they handle adversity. He remembered seeing—and hearing—a woman scream at a candidate at a Fourth of July parade four years ago and "he just smiled like it was nothing and kept waving."

University of Iowa Professor Peverill Squire said the state is so important in the presidential election because of its primacy in the political calendar, a positioning that leads to a lot of time and effort expended by the candidates in the Iowa caucuses.

At the caucuses, participation is key. "Because it's a caucus, you have to physically show up, sit with fellow party members and publicly identify yourself with your preference by where you sit so that you may be counted," said Larry Bird, a curator at the National Museum of American History in Washington.

Bird said the Iowa caucus "places a premium on participation and organization. It isn't a matter of buying time for campaign commercials . . . It's a matter of having people show up for you as a candidate."

Iowa has used the caucus system since it became a state in 1846. The only time Iowa had a primary election was April 10, 1916, and 25 percent of registered voters participated.

Despite the long history of Iowa caucuses, it was only in the latter part of the 20th century that outsiders paid much attention to them—and even then the state's strategic importance came about unintentionally.

At the Democratic National Convention in 1968, there was widespread dissent with the nomination of Hubert Humphrey, who did not win any of the contested primaries. The leaders of the Democratic Party then formed the McGovern-Fraser Commission to help unify the party and ensure that future nominations would accurately reflect overall party opinion. The commission adopted a system of proportional representation in which state parties had to follow rules and engage in a process open to all Democrats.

Iowa's strategic position at the forefront of all the other caucuses came about unintentionally.

Arthur Sanders, a professor at Drake University, explained that Iowans picked the specific date of the caucus "because of the availability of the site they wanted to use."

In 1972, George McGovern and his campaign manager, Gary Hart, thought that participating in the Iowa caucus might help their campaign because those would be the first formal results issued before the New Hampshire primary.

McGovern's capture of the Iowa caucuses gave a boost to his campaign that he carried to the party's nomination.

Then in 1976 President Jimmy Carter adopted the same strategy and won the presidency.

From that point on, presidential contenders and the media have paid attention to Iowa.

Ralph Christian, a historian at the State Historical Society of Iowa, said, "The 1988 (caucus) was the one I'll always remember because I went to my precinct in the inner city of Des Moines and we've got the Japanese press covering our caucus meeting. Satellite trucks lined the streets."

Iowa Caucus*

WIKIPEDIA, 2004

Process

The Iowa caucus operates very differently from the more common primary election used by most other states. The caucus is generally defined as a "gathering of neighbors." Rather than going to polls and casting ballots, Iowans gather at a set location in each of Iowa's approximately 2,000 precincts. Typically, these meetings occur in schools, churches, or libraries. The caucuses are held every two years, but the ones that receive national attention are the presidential preference primaries held every four years. In addition to the voting, the caucuses are used to discuss each party's platform and issues such as voter turnout.

The Iowa caucus is less binding than the first-in-the-nation New Hampshire primary because Iowan caucus-goers elect delegates to county conventions, who, in turn, elect delegates to district and state conventions where, ultimately, the national convention delegates are selected. The term "caucus" used in this sense is believed to be a Native American word meaning "a meeting of tribal leaders."

The Republicans and Democrats each hold their own set of caucuses subject to their own particular rules that change from time to time. Participants in each party's caucuses must be registered with that party. Participants can change their registration at the caucus location. Additionally, 17-year-olds can participate, as long as they will be 18 years of age by the date of the general election. Observers are allowed to attend, as long as they do not become actively involved in the debate and voting process.

Republican Party Process

The Republican caucuses are a straw poll where each voter places his or her vote in a hat (by secret ballot). The non-binding results are tabulated and reported to the media and the state party where delegates are later chosen.

Democratic Party Process

The process used by the Democrats is somewhat more complicated. Caucus-goers form into "preference groups," where their candidate preferences become public. For roughly 30 minutes, attendees try to convince their neighbors to support their candidates. Participants indicate their support for a particular candidate by standing in a designated area of the caucus site.

After 30 minutes, the electioneering is temporarily halted and the number of votes for each candidate is counted. The supporters of any candidate who doesn't have enough supporters to be "viable" will then have to find a viable candidate to support or simply choose to abstain. This viability level is currently set at 15% of the number of attendees at the caucus site. Consequently, for a candidate to receive any delegates from a particular precinct, he or she must have the support of at least 15% of that precinct. This causes the caucuses, unlike primaries, to favor front-running candidates.

From here, the caucus-goers have roughly another 30 minutes to support one of the remaining candidates or choose to abstain. When the voting is closed, a final head count is conducted, and each precinct proportionally apportions county delegates for each candidate who later attend a county convention.

The delegates chosen by the precinct then go to a later caucus, the county convention, to chose delegates to the district convention and state convention. At the district convention, the delegates assign 29 of the actual delegates to the National Convention from Iowa. At the state convention, the other 16 delegates are chosen. Delegates to each level of convention are not bound to vote for their chosen candidate and can switch allegiance.

---

* This article is licensed under the Free Documentation License. It uses material from the Wikipedia article "Iowa Caucus."

2004 Process

In 2004, the meetings ran from 6:30 P.M. until approximately 8:00 P.M. on January 19, 2004. The county convention is on March 13, the district convention on April 24, and the state convention on June 12. Delegates may change their votes based on further developments in the race; for instance, in 2004 the delegates pledged to Gephardt who left the race after the precinct caucuses will choose a different candidate, perhaps based on instructions from Gephardt.

The number of delegates each candidate receives eventually determines how many state delegates from Iowa that candidate will have at the Democratic National Convention. Iowa sends 56 delegates to the DNC out of a total 4,366.

Of the 45 delegates chosen through the caucus system, 29 are chosen at the district level. Ten delegates are at-large delegates, and six are "party leader and elected official" (PLEO) delegates; these are assigned at the state convention. There are also 11 other delegates, eight of whom are appointed from local Democratic National Committee members, two are PLEO delegates and one is elected at the state Democratic convention. The group of 45 delegates are pledged to a candidate; the group of 11 are unassigned.

Overview of the Primary Process[2]

BY CHRIS NAMMOUR
PBS ONLINE NEWSHOUR, DECEMBER 15, 2003

A common misconception about the primary election process is that votes are cast directly for candidates. In reality, they are cast in favor of delegates who will represent the candidates at the national conventions where they vote to select the party's presidential nominee.

The primary process was born from the desire of national and state parties to generate voter participation and grassroots mobilization. Traditionally, delegates who chose the presidential candidates were themselves chosen by caucus—more informal town hall meetings.

Primary elections were first held in a limited number of states in 1912, but did not really take hold until the latter half of the century. Reforms during the 1968 and 1972 Democratic national conventions encouraged the proliferation of primaries, and by the 2004 elections over 40 states will be holding primaries.

Party delegates are allocated to each state according to population size. Since the population is always shifting, so is the number of delegates assigned to particular states. The Democratic National Convention plans on having 4,317 total delegate votes for the 2004 primary. The Republican National Convention will include 2,512 delegate votes.

In the Democratic primaries, delegates are won on a state-by-state basis and are awarded proportionally by the number of votes the candidates receive. For example, if a state has 50 delegates and Candidate X gets 60 percent of the votes in that state primary, then Candidate X will receive 30 delegates.

While some Republican state parties also use this form of proportional representation, others use a winner-take-all approach, or some combination of the two methods.

This election cycle, the Republican primaries are expected to be a formality, leading to the nomination of President Bush for reelection at the party convention in late August 2004. The last incumbent to compete in his party's primaries—President Clinton in 1996—also ran unopposed and captured every delegate.

In the 1980 primaries, President Carter faced a determined rival in Sen. Ted Kennedy of Massachusetts, but went on to beat him by a 2-1 margin. In fact, the only sitting president to ever lose his party's nomination race was Franklin Pierce in 1856.

---

2. Article by Chris Nammour from Online NewsHour (December 15, 2003). Copyright © 2003 MacNeil-Lehrer Productions. Reprinted with permission of the publisher.

A key aspect of the primary system is that the elections are not held on the same day (like the general election) but are staggered over a period of months, from January to June. As the convention date approaches, the public generally gravitates toward the front-runners who have proven to be strong candidates. Usually, once the nomination is out of reach, opponents will drop out rather than waste money or political capital on a lost cause.

One result of this staggered schedule is that states with early primaries are extremely important to the candidates. A politician who does well early on is seen as a sure bet to supporters and potential campaign donors, while those who do not do as well will typically see their support wither and their funds evaporate.

New Hampshire and Iowa use this to their advantage. New Hampshire law dictates the primary must be held a week before any other primary, and Iowa law states the Iowa caucus must be held eight days before the New Hampshire primary. First-in-the-nation status carries benefits.

"Front loading" ... has been criticized heavily as under-mining the purpose of the primaries.

"It means more pork spending," said Andy Smith, director of the University of New Hampshire Survey Center. "New Hampshire is ranked 8th in the country in earmarked spending. There are a lot of politicians in the House and Senate with presidential aspirations who want to make friends with New Hampshire."

In a bid to counteract the disproportional influence of northern New Hampshire and Iowa, several Southern states banded together in 1988 to hold their primaries on the second Tuesday in March. This date came to be known as "Super Tuesday."

Other states eventually caught on to the Super Tuesday strategy, scheduling their primaries in groups. In some election years, this creates several Super Tuesdays. Due to the sheer number of delegates, these key primary dates have earned the reputation of making or breaking a candidate.

In the 2000 election, former New Jersey Sen. Bill Bradley conceded the Democratic nomination to former Vice President Al Gore shortly after a crushing 16-state defeat on Super Tuesday. Arizona Sen. John McCain fared only slightly better, managing to win a few northern states but losing the delegate-rich California, New York, and Ohio in one blow to future President Bush.

This "front loading"—the phenomenon of states holding their primaries in large groupings so early in the year—has been criticized heavily as undermining the purpose of the primaries.

Some argue that because front loading dramatically shortens the primary election calendar, it restricts candidates from spending much time on campaigning and instead emphasizes big money fund raising and media blitzes.

"Candidates aren't going to have a chance to effectively campaign," said Smith. "They make a cursory, shallow visit to the state. It's a television-tarmac campaign where they fly into the airport and then leave."

The current 2004 primary calendar indicates there will be several Super Tuesdays—this time starting in February, in addition to the customary first and second Tuesdays in March.

Granite State Tradition Forces Pols to Campaign Face to Face[3]

BY JACK SPILLANE
PORTSMOUTH HERALD, JANUARY 25, 2004

Everyone knows New Hampshire has long had the nation's first-in-the-nation primary, but less well known is the fact the Granite State also claims to have been the first state to come up with the idea of a national political convention and to be the state where the Republican Party was formed.

Some local historians even go so far as to claim it was a New Hampshire political type who first exclaimed, "This man should be president," during a visit by Abraham Lincoln to the mill city of Nashua.

New Hampshire Secretary of State Bill Gardner says it's all part of the tradition of town meeting, largest Legislature in the nation (400 members), fascination with elective politics in which the state's residents aren't happy voting for someone until they've met them personally four or five times.

"It's a very political culture here," said Gardner, a student of history and author of "Why New Hampshire?," a popular history of the primary that was just released.

"I think it probably stems from the time when colonial governors wouldn't allow the towns their own representatives.

So, when voters on Tuesday decide between Howard Dean, John Kerry, John Edwards, Wesley Clark, Joe Lieberman, Al Sharpton, and a host of amateurs who also placed their names on the ballot, they'll once again be making New Hampshire's history the nation's history.

Small State, Big Influence

How did one of the nation's smallest states, both in population and geography, secure such an influential place in the way the country picks presidents? Largely by accident, according to Gardner.

In 1905, when the progressive movement was widespread across the country, Wisconsin started the first primary and Indiana and Michigan also had early primaries, but by 1920, the other states had either moved their primaries to later in the year or gone back to the caucus system.

---

3. Courtesy of the *Portsmouth Herald.*

For the next 50 years, New Hampshire had the first-in-the-nation primary to itself and nobody really cared. Party bosses still largely picked the nominees in those days, and New Hampshire's quirky tradition of voting for its delegates was seen as just that: a quirky Yankee tradition.

And then came Gen. Dwight Eisenhower.

In 1952, largely on the basis of a good showing in the New Hampshire primary, the hero of World War II defeated "Mr. Republican," Ohio Sen. Robert Taft 50 to 39 percent and ultimately won the nomination from the party insider.

The New Hampshire primary was important for the first time, but its stature was only just beginning. By 1968, television had become the pervasive power in American communication and it turned its attention to anti-war Sen. Eugene McCarthy's insurgent New Hampshire primary campaign against embattled President Lyndon Johnson.

Sen. McCarthy only polled 42 percent of the vote to President Johnson's 50 percent (and he was a write-in) but the Minnesota senator did better than expected and got big headlines.

"It was television that really changed the primary," Gardner said. "In some respects, it was 1968 that brought the biggest changes for the primary and changed the nation, too."

In 1972, another anti-war senator, George McGovern, polled 37 percent to Maine Sen. Edmund Muskie's 46 percent but like Mr. McCarthy, he won the expectations game by doing better than expected.

Primary Upsets

After 1968 and 1972, the reputation for the New Hampshire primary for upsetting favored candidates was so established presidential aspirants were loathe to ignore it. That's when the effort to topple New Hampshire from its primary status started.

In 1976, a largely unknown former Georgia governor and peanut farmer—Jimmy Carter—came to New Hampshire early and often. He stayed overnight at the homes of no less than 70 state residents in his effort to wrest a primary victory from better known candidates like Morris Udall and Birch Bayh.

That's also the year when then former California governor Ronald Reagan, who at the time was considered a right-wing extremist, nearly defeated incumbent President Gerald Ford. He lost the primary 50 to 49 percent and went on to be elected president four years later, when he unexpectedly crushed former CIA director George H. W. Bush.

But it was Carter, coming from obscurity to win the 1976 primary, that earned New Hampshire its reputation for being a place where an outsider, an unknown underdog, actually stood a chance of winning.

Gardner calls President Carter, along with former Colorado Sen. Gary Hart and former President Clinton, the prototypical New Hampshire primary candidates. They may not have won the primary, but they used the one-on-one politics it demands to go from being little-known lawmakers from out-of-the-way places to powerful forces in American politics.

> *Most big states couldn't organize a primary as quickly as a small state.*

"Jimmy Carter was like a fringe candidate," said Gardner, who has been secretary of state in New Hampshire for 28 years. He remembers people referring to him derisively in the Statehouse corridors as "that guy who calls himself Jimmy.

"The real New Hampshire primary is in the spring and the fall the year before the election," he said. "That's when you go into people's homes and meet them. If someone comes into New Hampshire with a lot of money and a political entourage, it doesn't necessarily work here."

Power Plays

By 1972, other states, not to mention party insiders, began to envy the inordinate influence a small state like New Hampshire had on the election of a president (not to mention the beneficial effects on the local economy) and a spate of them tried to usurp the Granite State's primary.

Florida tried to lure them to a warmer campaign season, and Delaware and Michigan to states seen as more representative of the country as a whole (New Hampshire has one of the least urban and smallest minority populations in the nation), but they were all rebuffed through either their own incompetence or New Hampshire's persistence. Even party leaders have never succeeded in establishing a series of regional primaries rotating which section of the country would go first.

In 1975, New Hampshire passed a law that allows its secretary of state to schedule its primary at the last minute a week before the primary of any other state. Though Pennsylvania is already talking about challenging New Hampshire in 2008, state leaders are confident New Hampshire's rule will allow it to stay first: Most big states couldn't organize a primary as quickly as a small state, and of the small states, New Hampshire already has the tradition, they say.

Former state Rep. Jim Splaine, the Portsmouth Democrat who sponsored the state's first-in-the-nation law, said even many losing candidates feel having a small state with a tradition for retail politicking is better than letting money take over in advertising-driven campaigns in bigger states.

"Even the losing candidates will tell you they learned so much from us because in New Hampshire you have to talk and campaign with people rather than talk and campaign to people," he said.

Splaine said too much of American politics has become about advisors telling people how to talk, how to gesture and what positions are popular.

"Candidates are being overly coached," he said. "In someone's living room, you have to be genuine."

Long-shots Get Their Day

Since New Hampshire passed its first-in-the-nation law, the tradition of long-shots having a chance in the New Hampshire primary has continued.

After a better than expected showing in the Iowa caucuses, Gary Hart came from nowhere to beat Vice President Walter Mondale, 37 percent to 28 percent in 1984. In 1988, Vice President George H. W. Bush, after losing Iowa, came back and beat Senate Minority Leader Bob Dole in just one week, 38 percent to 28 percent.

In 1992, Arkansas Gov. Bill Clinton finished second to Massachusetts Sen. Paul Tsongas, 33 percent to 24 percent but because he came back from almost being eliminated by the Gennifer Flowers scandal, it was seen as a victory. In 1996, political commentator Pat Buchanan upset Bob Dole 27 percent to 26 percent and in 2000, Arizona Sen. John McCain upset then–Texas Gov. George W. Bush 48 percent to 30 percent.

Events to Images

Gardner said New Hampshire does not claim to be unique.

This year, even though Howard Dean was just as good, if not better at the retail politicking as John Kerry, the television focus on Dean's angry speech in Iowa may trump all other events, he said.

That happens in New Hampshire as elsewhere, such as when TV caught Ronald Reagan yelling "I paid for this microphone!" in a Nashua auditorium or Ed Muskie looking like he was crying on the steps of the New Hampshire state capitol. Those events go beyond retail politicking and can define a candidate's image, Gardner acknowledged.

But by and large, the retail politicking of New Hampshire's primary works well, he said. Though there are other small states where a first-in-the-nation primary might be OK, none of them have the Yankee tradition for first-hand, examine the candidate politics that New Hampshire does, Gardner argued.

"What makes New Hampshire unique is the political culture here. We believe the candidates who come here are better leaders later for having experienced it."

From The National Party Conventions

Function, History, and the Role of the Delegates[4]

CONGRESSIONAL DIGEST, OCTOBER 2000

National party conventions mark the turning point in the presidential campaign from the primary season to the general election. Every four years, delegates from State political parties gather at the Democratic and Republican National Conventions to nominate their party's choice for President and Vice President.

In 2000, there were about 2,100 delegates to the Republican Convention, held in Philadelphia from July 31 through August 3, and 4,300 delegates to the Democratic Convention, held in Los Angeles from August 14 through 17.

Purposes of Conventions

The conventions serve several important official and unofficial purposes:

- They ratify the choice for presidential nominee that the voters made during the primaries, and the nominee's choice for a running mate.

- They provide a forum for the adoption of the party platform, a document that serves as a declaration of the party's principles and positions on major issues.

- They unite and energize the party faithful as the candidates head into the fall campaign.

- They give parties an opportunity to showcase current and future leaders.

- They enable the parties and the nominees to connect with a broader national audience and communicate their messages through television and other media.

How Conventions Have Evolved

Before the 1830s, U.S. presidential candidates were selected by caucuses of the parties' representatives in Congress and State legislatures, or in State conventions. The first party conventions occurred in 1831, when the National-Republican (later Whig) and

---

4. Article from *Congressional Digest*, October 2000. Copyright © Congressional Digest Corp. Reprinted with permission.

Democratic parties met separately to choose their candidates to run for the presidency in 1832. The National-Republican Party picked Henry Clay, while the Democrats renominated President Andrew Jackson.

From the 1830s until the mid-twentieth century, it was common for the parties to have "brokered conventions." These were high-drama events, in which the presidential nomination was often up for grabs and rival factions met in "smoke-filled rooms" to negotiate party decisions.

When the process became deadlocked, the parties were forced to turn to a relatively unknown, or "dark horse," compromise candidate. This was the case in 1920, when Warren G. Harding became the Republican nominee and in 1924, when John W. Davis was named the Democratic candidate after 103 ballots.

The reason for the brokered conventions was that State delegations were chosen and controlled by State party leaders. "Less than 100 men in any convention really dictate what occurs," said Demo-

> ### *With the parties' presidential nominees determined months in advance of the conventions, the gatherings are widely seen as scripted, predictable, and "made for TV."*

cratic Party boss Ed Flynn of the Bronx, New York, in 1948.

The make-up of convention delegates didn't change significantly until the 1970s and 1980s, when the parties opened up the delegate selection process to include more women, minorities, and young people. The Democratic Party now requires that each State's delegation be equally divided between men and women.

Party platforms have also evolved over the years in the role they play in election year politics. Though they are not binding documents, they offer insights into philosophical differences between the two parties and the influence of their standardbearers.

At times, platforms have been the basis for future government actions, and some of the great issues of American history have been debated at the conventions. These include the Republican Party's opposition to slavery (in 1856), the Democratic Party's division over civil rights (in 1948), and the conflict over Vietnam (1968).

The process for choosing a vice presidential nominee has also changed over the years. The last open contest for a vice presidential running mate was at the Democratic Convention in 1956, when Senator Estes Kefauver of Tennessee won a close second-ballot victory over Massachusetts Senator John F. Kennedy to be on the ballot with presidential nominee Adlai Stevenson.

Media Coverage

Today, with the parties' presidential nominees determined months in advance of the conventions, the gatherings are widely seen as scripted, predictable, and "made for TV."

But while the television networks used to provide "gavel-to-gavel" coverage, today they broadcast only selected highlights, such as the keynote address and the nominees' acceptance speeches. Prime-time coverage of convention proceedings dropped from 90 hours in 1968 to less than 30 hours in 1992. The networks also spend more time cutting away from the speeches to inject their own commentary or to interview party leaders. With the advent of cable television news, however, viewers can tune into ongoing live coverage if they want to see more of the proceedings.

The 2000 conventions might be called the first real "Internet conventions" in that there were countless websites devoted to the week's events, maintained by the media, the parties, the candidates, and other organizations with a stake in the outcome.

Booths belonging to dozens of dot-com companies lined an "Internet Alley" at the Republican convention and an "Internet Avenue" at the Democrats' gathering. The pervasiveness of cellular phones, laptops, pagers, and other high-tech equipment at this summer's meetings required the installation of wiring systems not needed just four years ago.

At future conventions, however, today's communications technology no doubt will be shown to have been in its infancy, as it is replaced by even more sophisticated electronic systems.

Delegate Profiles

Despite these changes in the nominating process and how it is covered by the media, conventions remain a distinctly American tradition, with no counterpart in other Western democracies. And they hold special meaning for the delegates who attend them.

Convention delegates all have some kind of experience in electoral politics. At most conventions, more than two-thirds have held public office or have played some official party role. Usually more than half have attended at least one previous convention. Democrats provide for a category of "superdelegates" made up of members of the House and Senate, governors, and members of the Democratic National Committee. Instead of superdelegates, Republicans award States a specific number of "at-large" delegates of their own choosing.

IV. Money in Politics

Editor's Introduction

Money has been a major component of political campaigns since the 19th century, when candidates for office first took an active role in their own campaigns. Those with political aspirations needed to pay for travel expenses, advisers, and advertisements, among other things; and the well-financed candidate has historically possessed a distinct advantage over a less prosperous opponent. In recent years, with the polarization of the electorate and a constantly expanding media, campaigns have become more and more expensive, making it necessary for politicians to raise ever larger sums to finance them.

When politicians become dependent on campaign contributors for their electoral survival, they can often neglect the needs of constituents as they render themselves beholden to financiers rather than voters. In addition, the more money that is involved, the more opportunity there is for malfeasance or simply the perception of malfeasance. For instance, some viewed unregulated "soft money"—contributions from groups and individuals independent of political parties or campaigns—as a danger to the integrity of the system, since individuals and groups were free to make unlimited contributions in return for increased access and influence. Many found the system's excesses offensive and unseemly, and Congress acted. After years of debate and resistance from the president, the McCain-Feingold bill was passed by Congress, signed by President George W. Bush, and affirmed by the courts. Nevertheless, though McCain-Feingold is now the law of the land, critics still view it as antithetical to the Constitution's freedom of speech protections. These critics reason that campaign contributions are forms of political speech and therefore ought not to have limits imposed on them.

The bill, sponsored by Republican Senator John McCain of Arizona and Democratic Senator Russ Feingold of Wisconsin, has numerous implications for the future of the political process. This chapter will examine those implications while providing a general overview of how the system currently works and how we can expect it to change over time. David G. Savage for the *Los Angeles Times* describes how McCain-Feingold will alter the electoral landscape; Sharon Cohen, for the *Associated Press*, takes a revealing glimpse into the endless fund-raising required to finance election campaigns; and Frederick H. Lowe examines how the Internet, through small Web donations, is revolutionizing how politicians raise money.

Many critics agree that McCain-Feingold does not go far enough in limiting money's influence on the political process. Some have suggested that radio and television broadcasters should provide free air time to candidates running for office. Free air time, its proponents argue, would even the playing field between incumbents, who have a much easier time raising money, and their challengers, while enabling the candidates to get out their message with more detail and nuance than can be achieved through the 30-second sound bites that currently dominate political advertising. In this section Matt Farrey presents the case for free air time, while John Samples and Adam Thierer of the Cato Institute offer a counter argument. David Callahan for the *Washington Monthly* describes how money in forms other than campaign contributions can influence politics; the think tank, Callahan notes, has become a major outlet for politically motivated money.

High Court Upholds Most of Campaign Finance Law[1]

BY DAVID G. SAVAGE
LOS ANGELES TIMES, DECEMBER 11, 2003

The Supreme Court struck a blow Wednesday against the "growing evil . . . of big money" in American politics, ruling that Congress could stop the free flow of cash from corporations, unions, and the wealthy to fund political parties and buy campaign-style broadcast ads.

The 5-4 decision upheld nearly all of last year's broad campaign finance reform law, calling it a modest effort to ensure that the political system responds to the interests of ordinary voters, not just to those with the most money.

It was the most significant campaign-funding ruling since such laws were enacted in the post-Watergate era of the 1970s.

The law passed by Congress last year banned unlimited donations, known as "soft money," from individuals, corporations, and labor unions to political parties. Those donations—often reaching six figures or more—had come to dominate the fundraising process. The law also imposed limitations on political advertising by special interest groups.

The justices Wednesday called the McCain-Feingold act—named for its chief Senate sponsors, Republican John McCain of Arizona and Democrat Russell D. Feingold of Wisconsin—only "the most recent federal enactment designed to purge national politics of . . . the pernicious influence of big money campaign contributions." It will "protect the integrity of the political process," they concluded, by cutting the connection between large donations and political power.

But in one of four dissents, Justice Antonin Scalia said: "This is a sad day for the freedom of speech." Why, he asked, should a court obliged to protect free speech "smile with favor upon a law that cuts to the heart of what the 1st Amendment is meant to protect: the right to criticize the government."

Election law reformers celebrated the majority's ruling Wednesday.

"The toxic link between donors who write six-figure checks and people in power at the highest levels of government has been severed," said Chellie Pingree, president of Common Cause, a Washington-based political watchdog group.

---

1. Article by David G. Savage from the *Los Angeles Times* December 11, 2003. Copyright © *Los Angeles Times*. Reprinted with permission.

A reluctant President Bush signed the bill into law last year, and on Wednesday, White House reaction to the ruling was muted. It "will help bring some clarity to the process," Press Secretary Scott McClellan said.

The Democrats who are seeking to replace Bush were more enthused. "McCain-Feingold is a very important first step toward the sweeping campaign reform this country really needs," said former Vermont Gov. Howard Dean. "I'm glad the Supreme Court upheld the constitutionality of this law." While Wednesday's ruling sweeps aside legal doubts about the measure, its impact remains in question. Large amounts of cash will continue to pour into the political system, but the sources and flow are likely to be different.

In the 1996 election, for example, both President Clinton and his challenger, then–Senate Majority Leader Bob Dole (R-Kan.), tapped big donors for contributions to their parties. This money in turn paid for ads that boosted their campaigns.

This year, Bush is raising record amounts for his 2004 reelection campaign, but he is doing so by collecting individual contributions of

---

"McCain-Feingold is a very important first step toward the sweeping campaign reform this country really needs."—Howard Dean, former Vermont governor

---

$2,000 or less, the new legal limit. Dean, the Democratic front-runner, also is raising large amounts of money—mainly through small contributions gathered via the Internet.

The Bipartisan Campaign Reform Act of 2002, McCain-Feingold's official name, was intended to close the "twin loopholes of soft money and bogus issue advertising that have virtually destroyed our campaign finance laws," said Justices John Paul Stevens and Sandra Day O'Connor, quoting one of its Senate sponsors.

In upholding the law, the justices looked back to history. Money limits for federal campaigns are neither a new idea nor a suspect notion, they said, citing the Progressive Republicans of the early 20th century. Led by President Theodore Roosevelt, Congress in 1907 barred corporations from using their treasury funds to support candidates for federal offices. A similar ban on union funding was added in 1947. And after the Watergate scandal, Congress limited individuals to giving no more than $1,000 to a candidate for a single campaign.

By the 1990s, however, the system had sprung leaks. And by the end of the decade, a vast amount of money was pouring through the holes in the election law system, the justices said.

In the 2000 election cycle, $498 million in soft money flowed into the Democratic and Republican national parties. Theoretically, those funds were supposed to be used for purposes unrelated to specific campaigns, but everyone knew that was not the case. The money allowed big donors to buy influence with the members of Congress and the president.

At the same time, corporations, unions, and rich individuals were funding broadcast ads that praised or attacked candidates. Often, they did so behind a facade of misleading names. For example, a group called "Citizens for Better Medicare" was, in fact, made up of the major drug companies; it ran ads opposing candidates who favored controls on drug prices, the court noted. Another group, called "Republicans for Clean Air," was in reality two brothers, Sam and Charles Wyly, who spent $25 million on ads supporting then–Texas Gov. George W. Bush during the Republican primaries.

Under the 1974 law that created the Federal Election Commission and first limited contributions to candidates, such ads were deemed illegal if they urged viewers, for example, to "Vote No on Jones" on election day. However, a legal loophole allowed sponsors to evade the restriction if they said something more general, such as: "Send a message to Jones that you don't like his stand against seniors." During the 2000 election, 130 groups spent an estimated $500 million on these phony issue ads.

Reformers in Congress were determined to close both the soft money and advertising loopholes.

McCain-Feingold forbids the parties and politicians from seeking or raising soft money. They may raise a lot of small money contributions from individuals, but none from corporations or unions.

And the law did away with the notion of "issue ads." Instead, if a broadcast ad appears within 60 days of a federal election and refers to a "clearly identified candidate," it is considered an "electioneering communication." The wealthy, companies, and unions are barred from running these ads, because they are essentially campaign contributions. However, the parties and candidates may run ads that are paid for with small, legal donations.

Throughout the congressional battle over the reform law, Sen. Mitch McConnell of Kentucky, the chamber's second-ranking Republican, argued that these restrictions violated the 1st Amendment and its ban on laws "abridging the freedom of speech." Because the money paid for speech about politics, and political speech is at the heart of democracy, all the restrictions should be struck down, McConnell said.

He sued in hopes of voiding the law, and he was joined by a series of groups including the Republican National Committee and the National Rifle Assn.

The free-speech argument may have proved too much. Had the court agreed with McConnell's free-speech claim, the justices would have faced the prospect that all the campaign laws dating back a century were unconstitutional.

Instead, the five-member majority relied on past rulings to conclude that the funding restrictions put at most a "limited burden" on speech. The law limits how much money is given and spent, not what is said, the court explained.

> **The law limits how much money is given and spent, not what is said.**

Moreover, members of Congress knew all too well the possible corrupting influence of big campaign contributions, the justices said. For that reason, the court said, it had a special duty to defer to the judgment of the lawmakers themselves.

"Congress has a fully legitimate interest in maintaining the integrity of federal officeholders and preventing corruption of the federal electoral process," the court said in *McConnell vs. Federal Election Commission.* "The overall effect of dollar limits on contributions is merely to require candidates and political committees to raise funds from a greater number of persons," the court added.

Besides Stevens and O'Connor, Justice David H. Souter, Ruth Bader Ginsburg, and Stephen G. Breyer formed the majority.

Scalia, in his dissent, argued that the funding limits made it harder for outsiders to voice their opposition, and harder for challengers to take on incumbents. Chief Justice William H. Rehnquist and Justices Anthony M. Kennedy and Clarence Thomas also dissented from much of the ruling. In all, the court's opinions and the dissents ran to more than 275 pages.

The court voided only one provision in the law, a ban on contributions from minors. Congress added the provision to prevent rich parents from evading the limits by giving extra contributions in the name of their children. But the court said there was no evidence of such evasions.

Despite their differences, the justices managed to produce a clear ruling on a complex law.

Earlier this year, a three-judge panel in Washington found itself hopelessly divided over the issue—and it produced a confused set of opinions that ran to 1,600 pages and decided almost nothing.

The Supreme Court justices were determined to issue both a definitive ruling and to do it this month, before the official opening of the 2004 election year. They also said they were "under no illusion" that the law upheld Wednesday would resolve all the problems of campaign funding.

"Money, like water, will always find an outlet," they said. "What problems will arise . . . are concerns for another day."

How We Choose[2]

By Sharon Cohen
The Associated Press, April 19, 2004

Pete DeFazio decided his political future one restless night, staring at the ceiling in the darkness, his mind racing with thoughts of one dreaded word.

Money.

He tossed and turned, his anxiety growing as he did the math in his head: $12,000–$13,000 a day. Seven days a week. Nine months straight.

DeFazio figured he'd have to raise about $3.5 million to run any kind of credible U.S. Senate race in his home state of Oregon—a campaign the congressman was set to announce the next day.

He had been through this drill before and he hated it—dialing for dollars all the time, even as he drove to the airport, flew on planes, waited in lounges, landed and headed to his next appointment.

"It's embarrassing and it's mind-deadening," he says. "It was so obsessive and consuming that often times I didn't know where I was headed to—I just had to spend so much time trying to raise the money."

The next day, DeFazio announced his surprise decision: He would not run for the Senate.

"I just couldn't afford to do that," he says. "Life is too short."

Money is the lifeblood of politics, and increasingly, it defines and dominates campaigns.

It gives rich candidates an instant edge. It makes politicians prisoners of the coffee-and-cocktail fund-raising circuit—time that could be used to do the work of government, or to engage voters who are not wielding checkbooks.

It fuels the constant barrage of costly TV ads that have become a staple of elections in an era where a 30-second commercial can define a life.

Critics complain the frantic scramble for money is corrosive and has turned elections into a carnival of slick consultants, pollsters, and soundbites. They say well-heeled contributors spread around enormous wads of cash in return for favors, corrupting the system.

But defenders say money is used to inform voters, and the dollars raised from grassroots fund-raising drives give Americans more of a say in deciding who will govern. And they say fund-raising on the Internet promises to bring even more people into the process.

Either way, money talks in politics and it's louder than ever.

---

2. Reprinted with permission of The Associated Press.

"The amount of money that it takes to run a presidential campaign is just absolutely mind-blowing," says Joe Scarborough, a former Florida congressman turned MSNBC talk show host. "It can't be healthy for this republic that you've got to raise $200 million to have a shot."

Many of President Bush's supporters think he could raise $200 million in his re-election bid; presumptive Democratic nominee John Kerry hopes to reach about $105 million by his party's convention this summer.

And that doesn't include the $74.6 million each candidate will receive in public financing for the fall race.

Already, the increasing price of politics has weakened the clout of big-money contributors—checks that once opened doors to power-brokers barely rate a thank-you note anymore, lost as they are in the blizzard of other donations.

Scarborough recalls running into supporters four years ago who had contributed $100,000 or more to Bush or the Republican Party, but couldn't wangle invitations to the inaugural balls.

With that kind of donation 25 years ago, he says, "you'd have had the president's phone number in the Oval Office."

Not everyone laments the high cost of campaigns.

The price tag for selecting a president is still a bargain, considering it's the most powerful office in the world, argues Patrick Basham, a senior fellow at Washington's Cato Institute, which advocates limited government.

"We spend more on renting movies and buying frozen yogurt than we do per capita on politics," he says.

And this year there will be new boundaries on spending in federal campaigns.

This is the first election cycle since the U.S. Supreme Court upheld a ban on "soft money," which ended the common practice of corporations, labor unions, and others writing fat checks to the national Democratic and Republican parties. In the 2002 elections, the two parties raised nearly a half-billion dollars in "soft money."

The new ban, long championed by Sens. John McCain, R-Ariz., and Russ Feingold, D-Wis., is considered the most sweeping campaign finance law in 30 years.

Amount raised by George W. Bush and Al Gore in 2000 election, including federal matching funds, according to the Federal Election Commission: $279.9 million.

Amount spent by national political committees in 1936: about $14 million, or $170 million, adjusted for inflation.

"It has broken the corrupting nexus between huge contributors and federal officeholders," says Fred Wertheimer, president of Democracy 21, a campaign watchdog group. "The incentive for donors isn't there anymore."

Still, as much as $1.3 billion will be spent on political advertising in all races across the country this year, according to the Campaign Media Analysis Group. And in a nation of nearly 300 million people where candidates must rely on mass communi-

> *While the amounts are larger than ever, the marriage between dollars and democracy isn't exactly new.*

cations to spread their message, about 70 percent of the money will go to television.

Larry Sabato, director of the University of Virginia's Center for Politics, says that for all the worry about undue influence caused by this influx of cash, there is a positive side.

"It's also a means to a very good end—civic education," he says. "Without a lot of money, voters would not know some of the things they need to know"—such as the candidates' positions and their records.

And while the amounts are larger than ever, the marriage between dollars and democracy isn't exactly new.

William McKinley mastered it back in 1896 when he became the first presidential candidate to effectively tap big corporate campaign donors.

Guiding him was his street-savvy campaign manager Mark Hanna, who has been credited with a pithy political comment that seems to resonate more than ever today:

"There are two things that are important in politics," Hanna is quoted as saying. "The first is money—and I can't remember what the second one is."

Rich politicians have been around as long as the republic.

Nowadays, there are more of them, and their wealth is more public.

Average amounts raised by Democrats and Republicans in U.S. Senate races in 2002 general election, according to the Center for Responsive Politics: $5.8 million by incumbents, $1.9 million by challengers.

Amounts raised in House races in general election: $936,593 by incumbents, $274,794 by challengers.

Incumbents re-elected: 85 percent in Senate, 98 percent in House.

At least 42 of the 100 U.S. senators are members of the million-aires club—compared with 28 a decade ago, according to a report last year in *Roll Call*, the Capitol Hill newspaper. Because disclosure forms are imprecise, the newspaper says, the actual number is probably higher.

> *History . . . has proven that big money is no ticket to success.*

At the top of the list is Kerry, with an estimated $600 million, mostly due to his heiress wife's holdings.

A fat wallet can be an enormous asset, particularly for novices who can saturate the airwaves with TV ads.

Jon Corzine, for one, spent about $60 million of his Wall Street fortune to capture a U.S. Senate seat in New Jersey in 2000.

New York Mayor Michael Bloomberg, the billionaire former chief executive of a financial services information company, wrote himself a $73 million check to pave the way to City Hall three years ago.

His opponent, Mark Green, former New York City consumer affairs commissioner, says that's too rich for his blood.

"I raised and spent $16.5 million—that used to be real money," he says, noting he had 11,000 contributors listed in his telephone book–thick disclosure documents. "He (Bloomberg) had one piece of paper with one name."

Even a so-called millionaires amendment to the new campaign finance law, allowing candidates to increase the maximum they can raise from individuals when facing self-financed opponents, doesn't close the gap.

"My concern is in 20 years . . . most campaigns will be dominated by a billionaire who wants to buy it fair and square," Green says. "If that ever happens, women and men of talent without inherited or earned money are going to be squeezed out of our democracy."

Once in office, says DeFazio, the Oregon congressman who chose not to run for Senate in 1996, many of those millionaires "don't understand the needs of the middle class of average Americans, let alone poor people."

But history also has proven that big money is no ticket to success.

The political graveyard is littered with rich guys who pumped loads of cash into losing campaigns: Steve Forbes' bid for the presidency, Michael Huffington's race for senator from California, Tony Sanchez's run for Texas governor.

Average amounts raised for winning Democratic and Republican candidates in 2002 races, according to the Center for Responsive Politics: $966,670 for House, $5 million for Senate.

Of 29 federal candidates who spent $500,000 or more of their own money in 2002, only three won and they were not newcomers, according to the Center for Responsive Politics.

And sometimes being flush with donations doesn't do the trick, either.

James Rogan knows that. The former California congressman, one of the House managers in former President Clinton's impeachment trial, was at the center of the most expensive U.S. House race in history in 2000.

By the time the dust settled, he estimates, about $20 million came flooding into the nationally watched race, both in money he and his opponent raised and in funds spent by independent groups.

Rogan received more than 60,000 contributions, many from donors who saw the race as a referendum on impeachment. Toward the end, he started turning down money.

"What the extra money would have meant is you would have gotten seven pieces of mail instead of six," he says, "and instead of hearing 80 radio commercials, you'd hear 83."

Rogan even refused to cash a contribution from former President Bush.

"I said, 'If I can't win this race on $7 million, I'm not going to win it on $7 million and one thousand.'"

He framed Bush's check. And he lost the election.

"Philosophically," he says, "I just did not fit that district."

Eli Pariser is one of a new breed of political fund-raisers.

From a tiny office in his fourth-floor walk-up in midtown Manhattan, Pariser rakes in millions of dollars as head of the political action committee formed by MoveOn.org, a liberal group opposed to many of President Bush's policies.

For the 23-year-old Pariser, there's strength in numbers.

"People believe there's this huge ocean of money that is going into the presidential race and they say, 'What is my $25 going to do?'" he says. "When they know they're giving in conjunction with 10 or 20,000 people, all of a sudden you're talking about $250,000 or $500,000 or a million dollars, all coming together very quickly. That's very powerful."

In March, his political action committee, or PAC, pulled in $1 million in three days—the average donation was $44—to run an ad accusing Bush of being laggard in coming to grips with the dangers of terrorism.

Amount of money spent by all candidates in 1956, according to the Web site opensecrets.org: $155 million.

Amount spent in 1996, according to ThisNation.com: $4.2 billion.

And in the 2002 elections, the MoveOn PAC raised more than $4 million to help some 20 Democratic House and Senate candidates.

Pariser is far from alone in harnessing the Internet's power.

RightMarch.com, an umbrella site for conservative groups, was developed as a rapid response to MoveOn.org to raise money for newspaper ads that counter the liberal organization's message.

"We're fighting fire with fire," says William Greene, the founder.

The hands-down winner in the Internet fund-raising derby, of course, has been Howard Dean, the former Vermont governor whose presidential bid went down in flames even though he raised some $50 million, much of it from small donors who gave online.

"By giving money, they have crossed the line from spectator to participant," Sabato says. "There's no more important line in politics."

And yet contributing largely remains a province of the elite.

In the 2002 elections, 83 percent of donations $200 or more reported to the FEC came from less than one-tenth of 1 percent of the population, according to the Center for Responsive Politics.

The new bans on labor and business donations to the national political parties—and limits on other such donations—will now force candidates to scour even more for smaller contributions.

But there are plenty of other sources of money.

Political action committees still contribute to candidates. They represent every powerful lobbying group—doctors, drug manufacturers, trial lawyers, and unions—as well as advocates for single issues like abortion and gun control, and raised about $376 million last year, according to the FEC.

PACs, however, are limited by law in the size of their contributions and must register with the FEC. In this election year, another kind of advocacy group—the so-called 527 organization, named for a section of the tax code—has become more popular and controversial.

These tax-exempt "soft money" groups, independent of parties and campaigns, are not registered with the FEC. They can raise endless amounts of cash and have been eager to scoop up big dollars the parties used to get. Democrats have been quickest to capitalize on them, bolstered by huge contributors such as billionaire George Soros.

Some of the 527 groups have run anti-Bush TV ads, leading the president's campaign to accuse them of being in cahoots with Kerry—something that is forbidden under the law, and something the Democrat denies.

But clearly, donations that would have made their way to the political parties, pre-McCain-Feingold, are now going into the coffers of 527 groups.

"Under the First Amendment, it's virtually impossible to stop the flow of money," Sabato says. "You can reroute the flow. And that's what's happening again."

For more than 25 years, Larry Noble has tracked the money pipeline in the nation's capital.

He has watched from inside the government—as former FEC general counsel—and from the outside, in his present post as director of the Center for Responsive Politics.

He has seen how money has shaped, sometimes corrupted the democratic process—from the post-Watergate reforms that required disclosure of contributions to the era where seven-figure donations didn't raise an eyebrow to the newest laws aimed at curbing the excesses.

He says that even before these latest reforms, people were looking for loopholes.

For him, it's all part of a continuing dance.

"There's always going to be that power of money in politics, there's always going to be influence-buying," he says. "This is just a universal struggle. You try to make the system better. But you never reach a point where you're done."

Fundraising Crucial for U.S. Presidential Candidates[3]

By Stephanie Ho
VOANEWS.COM, January 14, 2004

U.S. presidential candidates have broken fundraising records as they head into the 2004 election year. Raising money to pay for election campaigns has become an essential part of American politics.

President Bush made headlines recently with news that during 2003, his campaign had already raised more than $130 million for his re-election bid. This figure broke a previous record of $100 million that he set in 2000.

The Democratic candidate with the most money, Howard Dean, raised more than $40 million in 2003, an amount that shattered the one-year record for Democratic party presidential campaign fundraising.

Candidates from either party can accept federal funds for their campaigns, but they must abide by spending limits. Mr. Bush, Mr. Dean, and another Democratic candidate, Senator John Kerry, have all opted out of the system. As the leading challenger, Mr. Dean still only has about one-fourth of the president's financial war chest. At a recent Democratic debate, he contended that he and his fellow candidates are at a serious disadvantage. "The front-runner in this campaign is George W. Bush, and all the powerful people who've given him millions of dollars and benefited from his policies," he said.

The importance of money is evident in the amount of time presidential candidates, including the incumbent president, spend fundraising.

At a fundraiser in Maryland in December, President Bush thanked donors, and said he hopes their financial support will translate into votes for him at the polls. "I want to thank you for your contributions," he said. "I also want to thank you for the contribution of time you're going to make."

Why does money matter? Steve Weiss, of the non-partisan Center for Responsive Politics, a group that tracks money in American politics and its effect on elections, says money helps improve a candidate's chances of success.

---

3. Article from the *VOANews.com*, January 14, 2004. Copyright © Voice of America. Reprinted with permission.

"In elections overall, roughly nine out of ten times, the candidate who spends the most money wins the elections," he said. "That's most often true in congressional elections, but the same principle applies to presidential elections. Money doesn't buy you elections, but it can go a long way to strengthening your candidacy."

Republicans historically have raised more money than their Democratic rivals. But Joe Sandler, a lawyer who served as in-house legal counsel for the Democratic National Committee for five years in the 1990s, says that has not stopped Democratic candidates from winning elections.

"We were vastly outspent in 1992, when we won the presidency," he said. "We were vastly outspent in 1996, when President Clinton was the first Democratic president to be re-elected in 40 years, and so—we need enough to be competitive. We don't have any illusions it will ever be at parity."

That underdog spirit is apparently driving Carol Moseley Braun, who was the only woman in a field of nine Democratic presidential candidates. Before she dropped out of the race, the former Illinois senator is reported to have raised only several hundred thousand dollars and was trailing in nationwide support.

"When you start off being different, you have to campaign differently," she said. "And we've done the best we can within the resources that we have to get around to the states that are involved in this process. I have done more with less money."

As states go through their own Democratic caucuses and primaries, candidates who lack electoral support will have trouble raising money and will be forced to quit the race.

"The ability to raise money, and fundraising itself, is hugely important. It signals a well-organized campaign," said Steve Weiss from the Center for Responsive Politics. "It shows strength and the enhanced ability to win an election. And it shows popular support as well. If you're not raising much money, it just doesn't bode well for your campaign in a number of respects."

Mr. Weiss, whose group tracks the influence of money in politics, says voters would be wise to not only pay attention to which candidates are raising the most money, but also to which groups or individuals may be contributing money, in hopes of influencing the various candidates.

Small Web Donations Have
Politicians Thinking Big[4]

BY FREDERICK H. LOWE
CREDIT CARD MANAGEMENT, DECEMBER 2003

Politicians still raise a fork on the rubber-chicken circuit, attend state fairs, march in parades, hold large rallies, and convene small meetings with supporters to raise money for their campaigns. But they increasingly are relying on credit card donations made over the Internet to fill their campaign coffers.

Whether the politician is running for city dogcatcher or the White House, many of them have Web sites that allow supporters to make campaign contributions in their pink bathroom slippers from their home computers.

"Credit card donations made over the Internet are the single biggest source of our funding," says David Swanson, campaign press secretary for U.S. Rep. Dennis Kucinich, a liberal Ohio Democrat and former Cleveland mayor seeking his party's nomination for president. "We do not accept money from corporate PACs (political action committees), and we do not accept rides on corporate jets. We need to reach as many people as possible for contributions, and the Internet is invaluable."

Kucinich for President Inc. raised $1.7 million during the third-quarter reporting period and $3.4 million since Kucinich launched his campaign, according to the Federal Election Commission. Swanson says 57% of Kucinich's total donations, or $1.9 million, have come from credit card donations made over the Internet.

Kucinich is not alone in relying heavily on card donations. Clark for President, retired Gen. Wesley K. Clark's campaign committee, has raised 66% of its campaign funds from credit card donations made over the Internet, a spokesperson says.

Clark, who launched his bid for the Democratic nomination for president in October, raised $3.4 million, according to the FEC. About $2.2 million came from credit card donations.

The FEC, through a series of advisory opinions, has allowed voters to make card donations over the Internet to their preferred candidate. The FEC delivered its most important ruling on this issue in an advisory opinion released on June 10, 1999, when it allowed candidates to qualify for federal matching funds for campaign contributions made over the Internet, according to Larry Noble, the FEC's former general counsel.

---

4. Article by Frederick H. Lowe from *Credit Card Management,* December 2003. Copyright © *Credit Card Management.* Reprinted with permission.

That action broke presidential fundraising wide open because the FEC dealt with the issue of electronic transfers, Noble says.

The Engine's Revving

Web-based card donations have been revving the political fundraising engine ever since. The day after U.S. Sen. John McCain, R-Ariz., won the New Hampshire Republican presidential primary in

> *Web-based card donations have been revving the political fundraising engine ever since.*

2000, he raised $6 million through Internet contributions. Albert Gore, the 2000 Democratic nominee for president, also accepted card donations over the Internet.

The candidates seeking the 2004 Democratic presidential nomination, however, have raised the visibility of this form of fundraising to headline-grabbing highs. In particular, Howard Dean, a physician and former Vermont governor, has been highly successful on the Web. Dean for America, Dean's campaign arm, raised $7.4 million over the Internet, half of the $14.8 million the campaign raked in during the third quarter, according to Convio Inc., an Austin, Texas, company that designed and operates Dean's Web site.

Convio also designed and operates Connecticut Sen. Joseph Lieberman's Joe for President Inc.'s Web site, but a Convio spokesperson says the firm is "verboten" from discussing it.

Since Convio opened Dean's Web site in April, his campaign has raised $11 million online. The success of online fundraising has been key in raising Dean's campaign visibility because money is, as the old cliché goes, the mother's milk of politics.

"He's gone from a nobody with no chance to the leading candidate, and the Internet has taken him there," says Phil Noble (no relation to Larry), president of Charleston, S.C.–based Internet political services firm PoliticsOnline. "Dean has made online fundraising central to his campaign."

The Democratic candidates' success with Web-based fundraising is more evolutionary than revolutionary, says Larry Noble, who is now executive director of the Center for Responsive Politics, a non-partisan organization in Washington, D.C., that tracks money in politics. Consumers who have become comfortable typing in their credit card numbers to pay for Web purchases don't have any problem using their cards to make online political contributions, he says.

Phil Kumnick, senior vice president of global partner solutions at Tempe, Ariz.–based merchant processor Vital Processing Services, which processes online card donations made to Dean, echoes that view. "They would rather make a contribution over the Internet than write a check and mail it," he says.

The growth in online contributions has spawned new business opportunities for processors and merchant acquirers. From July 2002 to July 2003, Vital recorded an increase of well over 40% in processing card donations for political candidates, Kumnick says. He adds that other companies, which he declined to name, are processing millions of card transactions involving political donations.

This growth area has attracted a lot of dabbling from various processors, but not specialization, according to Joe Kaplan, president and chief executive of Innovative Merchant Solutions, a merchant acquirer based in Calabasas, Calif.

San Francisco–based Wells Fargo & Co. processed Web-based donations for one of the candidates running for mayor of San Francisco last month. Wells also designed the candidate's Web site, but the bank declined to name the person.

"The credit card is another payment vehicle for political donations, and we are experienced in handling secure credit card payments on the Internet," says Debra Rossi, Wells Fargo executive vice president of business Internet services.

Few Checks or Debit Cards

Visa USA declined to discuss how much interchange it charges to accept a Web-based political donation made with a credit card, but Kumnick says it is treated as a card-not-present transaction. The Visa rate for such a transaction as of Aug. 1 was 1.85% of the sale plus 10 cents. If the acquirer verifies the cardholder's address, it realizes certain chargeback rights, he adds.

Political donations made over the Internet with a MasterCard qualify for MasterCard's Merit 1 interchange rate, according to Kumnick. That rate is 1.90% of the sale plus 10 cents.

Nearly 100% of online political donations are made with credit cards, says Phil Noble of PoliticsOnline. "No one talks about electronic checks or debit cards," he says.

The candidates seeking the Democratic nomination, however, differ in what card brands they accept. Kucinich, who considers himself the candidate of the working class, accepts Visa and MasterCard. Clark accepts Visa, MasterCard and American Express and so do the campaigns of U.S. Sens. John Edwards and John Kerry.

Donators to Al Sharpton 2004, the Rev. Al Sharpton's campaign organization, can make contributions using person-to-person electronic payments provider PayPal. A PayPal account either can be funded with a check or a credit card. The cost to accept a PayPal transaction is considerably lower than that of a card payment.

Kaplan, of Innovative Merchant Solutions, says card contributions are the most popular way to make a donation to a political candidate because they are the most efficient.

"If a person writes a check and mails it, the candidate has to wait for the check to arrive," he says. "The person also may forget to write the check. If a person wants to make a donation over the telephone, the telephone lines of a candidate's phone bank may be busy. Card donations are quick and secure."

An Edge for Democrats?

The acceptance of credit card donations may give an edge to the Democrats, who typically raise less than Republicans do. In an industry dominated by $2,000-per-plate black-tie dinners, Vital Processing's Kumnick says the average card donation to candidates is $80. Swanson, of Kucinich for President, says the average donation from the campaign's 44,149-member database of contributors is $75.39. Dean for America has raised 71% of its contributions from small donors or through small payments, says Convio.

"The normal Democratic or Republican campaign has been more like around 30% from small contributors," says the Convio spokesperson.

"Dean and Kucinich have managed to become less reliant on the superrich, which should make them more responsive to the needs of ordinary people."—**Matthew Rothschild,** *The Progressive*

Matthew Rothschild, editor of *The Progressive*, a liberal magazine based in Madison, Wis., praised Dean and Kucinich for their fundraising in an Oct. 17 editor's note.

"Dean and Kucinich have managed to become less reliant on the superrich, which should make them more responsive to the needs of ordinary people," Rothschild wrote.

To assuage concerns about online fraud, most of the presidential candidates make clear to individuals that their Web-based card donations will be secure transactions. For example, John Edwards's and U.S. Rep Richard Gephardt's Web sites prominently display the VeriSign Secure Site logo. Former U.S. Sen. Carol Moseley Braun's Web site explains that the Carol Moseley Braun for President 2004 campaign organization has partnered with Bank of America to guarantee "absolute security" of a donor's credit card information.

On most of the candidates' Web sites, supporters can contribute amounts ranging from $25 to $1,000. The minimum contribution is $5, and the maximum is $2,000.

Before a person can make a donation over the Internet to a candidate, he has to answer "yes" to a series of questions on the candidate's Web site. They are:

- I am not a foreign national who lacks permanent residence in the United States.

- This contribution is made from my own funds, and not those of another person.

- This contribution is not made from the general treasury funds of a corporation, labor organization, or national bank.

- I am not a federal contractor.

- This contribution is made on a personal credit card or debit card for which I have the legal obligation to pay, and is not made either on a corporate or business entity card or on the card of another person.

- I am at least 18 years old.

The questions are asked to meet FEC reporting guidelines, says Dan Hart, Convio's vice president of engineering.

But despite the growth of online credit card contributions, there are some concerns.

Larry Noble, of the Center for Responsive Politics, says people who donate online may not necessarily vote. And Swanson, of Kucinich's office, says soliciting campaign contributions over the Internet does not reach people who don't have computers. Kaplan, meanwhile, worries about chargebacks.

"What if a person makes a contribution to a candidate who loses?" he says. "Will he want his money back?"

It's a concern, but so far a minor one. As Campaign 2004 heats up, politicians of every persuasion are coming to an agreement that cards and the Web have widened the fundraising base.

Free Airtime: How to Use a Public Good for the Public Interest[5]

By Matt Farrey
National Civic Review, Summer 2003

The enactment of the Bipartisan Campaign Reform Act of 2002 (BCRA) was the most significant overhaul of the nation's campaign finance system in a generation. It bans unlimited contributions from labor unions, corporations, and wealthy individuals to political parties; and it requires that all campaign ads that air in the 60 days before an election—whether sponsored by candidates, parties, or outside groups—be paid for with disclosed and limited contributions. These are important reforms that will reduce the corrupting influence of money in politics and begin to restore public trust in our democratic institutions.

However, the BCRA is already being challenged in the courts and undermined by the Federal Election Commission, the federal agency that is supposed to enforce the new law. As of spring 2003, its effectiveness remains uncertain. But what's already clear is that even if the BCRA survives hostile fire from litigants and regulators, we'll still be left with a political system in which money rules. That's because the BCRA limits and controls the supply of big money in politics, but it does little to dampen the demand. It won't open up the democratic process to average Americans, or bring vibrancy to our political discourse. In the post-BCRA world, there might be less corruption in politics, but the competitive playing field of campaigns will still be heavily tilted toward candidates who are wealthy or who have access to special interest money.

More reform is desperately needed. One promising place to start is the Political Campaign Broadcast Activity Improvements Act, introduced in October 2002 by Senators John McCain, Russ Feingold, and Richard Durbin. This bill is the first step in what should be a refocusing of the long-term priorities of the campaign reform movement. The new emphasis should be on finding practical, achievable, innovative ways to open up a closed system. It should focus on providing resources to candidates who demonstrate the ability to raise a threshold amount of money from a broad base of small donors.

Campaign costs have been rising at a breakneck pace for the past generation, and the 2002 election was no exception. Last year, as usual, the biggest single campaign expense was the cost of broadcast television advertising. In 2002, candidates, parties, and issue groups spent more than $1 billion to communicate with voters over the airwaves. The Campaign Media Analysis Group estimates that $995.5 million was spent to air nearly 1.5 million political spots just in the top 100 media markets in the country. (This estimate does not include the nation's 111 smaller markets, several with high-spending races.) The 2002 figure is nearly double what was spent in the 1998 midterm congressional elections and even exceeds what was spent in the 2000 presidential election, which featured contested primaries for both major parties and an extremely tight general election.

Part of the reason for the increase in spending on television advertising is that broadcasters, who receive free and exclusive licenses to use the public's airwaves, jack up their advertising rates substantially in the weeks before election day. An Alliance for Better Cam-

---

The high cost of elections . . . produce campaigns characterized by a stark absence of competition, minimal public debate of the issues, and no real choices for voters.

---

paigns study of 38 stations in 22 media markets found that stations charged an average of 51.6 percent more for the typical political ad in the week before the 2002 election than they charged for the typical spot in the final week of August 2002, 10 weeks before election day. Some stations were especially egregious in their profiteering on democracy. For example, KTXL-TV in Sacramento, a Fox affiliate owned by the Tribune Company, charged candidates an average of $322 for a 30-second spot during the week of August 26 through September 1, 2002. During the week of October 28 through November 4, the average price paid for a candidate spot jumped to $1,129, an increase of 250 percent!

The consequences of the high cost of elections—driven by the high cost of television advertising—are clear. They produce campaigns characterized by a stark absence of competition, minimal public debate of the issues, and no real choices for voters. In the 2002 congressional elections, 99 percent of House incumbents who sought reelection were successful. The average margin of victory in a congressional race was 40 percentage points. The average amount spent to win a congressional race was $895,486, according to the Center for Responsive Politics. Because the price of entry is so high and because it is virtually impossible to defeat an incumbent, many potential challengers choose not to run at all. Moreover, an Alliance for Better Campaigns analysis of candidate expenditures in 41 contested House races (those with a margin of victory of 10 percent or less) found that the cost of political advertising accounted for 49.2 percent of the campaign spending in those races. At a price tag of almost $900,000 for a congressional race—nearly half of which will pay for television ads—the democratic process is effectively closed to most Americans.

The legislation that Senators McCain, Feingold, and Durbin introduced last fall seeks to address these problems in three ways. First, it requires the nation's 1,300 television stations and 13,000 radio stations to air a minimum of two hours per week of candidate issue discussion in the weeks before elections. Second, it would establish a system of broadcast vouchers that enables federal candidates who raised a threshold of small dollar donations to earn a reasonable amount of free advertising time on the broadcast station of their choice. The vouchers would be financed by a spectrum use fee on broadcast license holders, fixed at less than 1 percent of gross annual revenues. Finally, the bill would close loopholes in a 32-year-old law that is supposed to prevent stations from gouging candidates on their ad rates. By opening up the airwaves in these ways, the bill will begin to lower the price of entry to the democratic process. More candidates will have a chance to present their ideas to the public, new ideas may emerge, voters will see new faces, and we will have a more competitive and thus a more vibrant democracy.

More than 40 national organizations have endorsed the Political Campaign Broadcast Activity Improvements Act (known as the "McCain Feingold Durbin Broadcast Bill"), including Common Cause, the League of Women Voters, Public Citizen, the Alliance for Better Campaigns, U.S. PIRG, the AFL-CIO, AFSCME, the Communications Workers of America, the Sierra Club, the National Council of Churches, Rock the Vote, and the League of United Latin American Citizens. This coalition has also launched the Our Democracy, Our Airwaves Campaign, a nationwide public education and advocacy campaign to build support for these proposals. In addition to this national coalition, dozens of state-based civic groups and hundreds of citizen activists across the country are hosting public forums, collecting petition signatures, and educating their neighbors about the need to open up the democratic process. After the U.S. Supreme Court issues a ruling on BCRA, it is expected that the Senate Commerce Committee (chaired by Senator McCain) will hold hearings to consider the McCain Feingold Durbin Broadcast Bill. You can learn more about this legislation and sign up to receive regular updates about the campaign at *www.freairtime.org*.

The rallying cry of campaign reformers in the last decade has been that money is corrupting democracy. The BCRA was designed to take the biggest and most potentially corrupting checks out of the political process. But the fact remains that candidates still have to raise huge sums of money to run for office. So the money will continue to flow—it will just flow in different ways and in different directions than it did in the pre-BCRA world. The end result will still be a democratic process that's closed to those who are unable or unwilling to find ways to raise the money needed to wage a competitive campaign. For the past decade, campaign reform has been about limiting corruption by limiting money in politics. lt's now time for a new rallying cry, one that calls for opening up our political system to more candidates, more ideas, more choices. We should start by opening up our public airwaves and reinvigorating our democracy.

Subsidizing Soapboxes: McCain's Free Airtime for Politicians Bill[6]

By John Samples and Adam Thierer
Cato.org, September 24, 2003

The drive to regulate political speach did not end with the passage of the Bipartisan Campaign Reform Act in 2002. Sen. John McCain (R-Ariz.) and several congressional allies recently introduced the "Our Democracy, Our Airwaves Act of 2003," which would force broadcasters to provide "free" airtime to presidential and congressional political candidates and parties. Welcome to the age of subsidized soapboxes for politicians and the next major step toward full-blown taxpayer financing of elections.

The McCain bill would impose two major rules on broadcasters. One would require them to run 12 hours of "candidate-centered and issue-centered programming" in the six weeks prior to primary and general elections—without giving them any control over the 12 hours (half of which must occupy prime time). The second would create a voucher system for the purchase of airtime for political advertisements, financed by an annual spectrum-use fee on all broadcast license holders. In other words, if McCain's bill passes, stations will pay a tax to the federal government that would in turn finance a pool of voucher funds that politicians could turn around and spend to run ads on those same stations. And we're not talking small sums here. In 2004, the bill foresees giving candidates for Congress and the presidency $750 million worth of airtime.

McCain's free airtime proposal is based on outdated assumptions about the broadcast media and politics, and raises a number of constitutional concerns.

Supporters of free airtime say galloping TV ad rates have sent the cost of political campaigns soaring and have thus led to even more special interest influence over candidates. But a new study by MIT and Yale scholars shows that ad rates are not to blame for the increase in campaign spending over the last two decades. Further, the researchers uncovered 30 reputable social science studies that show financial contributions have no influence on roll call votes in Congress.

The free airtime measure rests upon the longstanding theory that the wireless broadcast spectrum should be a public resource, owned and regulated by the government at the whim of legislators

---

and regulators. But spectrum property rights can, and are, developing that will allow for the private management of the airwaves, including broadcast television and radio spectra. Besides being heavy handed, the McCain approach may soon be obsolete.

The proposal also raises serious First Amendment concerns. If McCain sought to control the editorial content of newspapers, everyone would immediately see the patent unconstitutionality of his proposal. Yet courts have said government regulation of broadcasting is different, largely because of spectrum scarcity. That rationale looks silly when Americans can receive hundreds of television channels from all manner of sources.

The McCain bill's proponents proclaim it is "in the public interest" to subsidize political campaigns. But as economic history has made clear, "public interest" regulation rarely has much to do with what the viewing public desires. Rather, such regulation has been employed as an excuse for politicians and industry interests alike to use regulation to achieve a variety of private ends.

While the public has very little say in shaping the politically defined public interest standard, consumers have made it clear what they demand in the video programming marketplace. Commercial television in America does reflect what the public really wants to see and hear.

What politicians are perhaps afraid to ask is: Do people really want to watch more campaign spots and politically oriented programming? "The notion that Americans are starving for more exposure to politics is cockeyed," says *Boston Globe* columnist Jeff Jacoby. "Americans have never been less interested in campaigns and elections." Recent polls say broadcasters have provided "about the right amount" or "too much" campaign coverage during recent election cycles.

McCain and friends want to solve problems that do not exist by overriding the editorial discretion of broadcasters. His free airtime proposal has no place in a market-driven digital media age where broadcasters give consumers the programs they want.

The Think Tank as Flack[7]

By David Callahan
The Washington Monthly, November 1999

On September 18, *The New York Times* ran a breathless front-page account of corporate propaganda. The Microsoft Corporation, we learned, had bankrolled a California think tank—ironically named the Independent Institute—to run full-page newspaper ads supporting Microsoft's claim of innocence in the face of federal antitrust charges. The ads took the form of a letter signed by 240 academic "experts" and purported to be a scholarly, unbiased view of why the government had gone overboard in its case against the company. According to the *Times* article, Microsoft had not only paid for the ads, but was in fact the single largest donor to the Independent Institute, a conservative organization that has been a leading defender of the company since it first came under fire from federal prosecutors.

This revelation has been an embarrassment both to Microsoft and to the Independent Institute, which claims to adhere to the "highest standards of independent scholarly inquiry." But the *Times* is another institution that should be embarrassed, trumpeting the story as a shocking exposé. To be sure, the article had timely elements, running on the eve of final arguments in the high profile Microsoft trial. But framed more broadly, the tale of right-wing think tanks propagandizing on behalf of their corporate masters is now many years old. What was truly remarkable about the *Times* story is that the paper has run so few similar stories and has failed to report on one of the most important ways in which corporate dollars seek to influence public policy.

Three mighty rivers of private money now help shape American politics. The first, and most familiar, is direct campaign contributions to political candidates and parties. Little mystery surrounds this giving. Unmistakably, these donations are naked attempts by corporations and other donors, like unions, to influence the political process. In the past quarter century, untold numbers of news stories have exposed this dark side of American democracy and efforts to dam the campaign spending river have long been underway.

The second great river of money goes to underwrite a vast lobbying apparatus in Washington and state capitals. Again, this is a river that flows largely in public view, thanks to the efforts of muckraking journalists and good government groups. The shop-

---

worn image of special interest lobbyists circling around federal and state legislators like buzzards is one reason why so many Americans distrust government.

The third river of private money flowing into politics is less well-known, but nearly as wide and deep as the other two. It is the money which underwrites a vast network of public policy think tanks and advocacy groups. Historically, much of this money—on both the left and the right—has come from foundations. For public policy organizations on the left and the center, this source of money remains dominant, with some funds also coming from unions. However, the big development of the 1990s is that conservative institutes have had spectacular new success in tapping business money to fund ideologically charged policy research.

> *Money . . . can buy scholars as well as politicians.*

Over the past 10 years, a huge influx of private sector money has allowed conservative think tanks and advocacy groups to grow by leaps and bounds. Not only are well-known organizations like CATO, the American Enterprise Institute, and the Heritage Foundation more flush with cash than ever, but giving by corporations and wealthy businessmen—all of which is tax-deductible—has underwritten the rise of a new generation of smaller and often brasher conservative think tanks like the Competitive Enterprise Institute (CEI) and the Reason Foundation. Corporate money has also fueled the explosive growth of dozens of state-based conservative think tanks, of which the Independent Institute is a prime example. In 1996, according to data I published in a report early this year by the National Committee for Responsive Philanthropy, the top 20 conservative think tanks spent $158 million, more than half of it contributed by corporations or wealthy businessmen.

Needless to say, hard-edged corporate executives like Bill Gates are not giving away money for nothing. They expect a return on their investment, and by and large they have gotten one. Corporate giving to right-wing groups has steadily increased as private sector leaders have seen the effectiveness with which conservative think tanks, and their armies of credentialed "experts," advance business interests in the political arena. Money, it turns out, can buy scholars as well as politicians.

The current gusher of corporate funding for right-wing policy work has its roots in the 1970s, when leading conservative thinkers appealed to corporations to fund intellectuals who supported their economic interests. In his 1978 book *Two Cheers for Capitalism*, Irving Kristol argued that corporations should make "philanthropic contributions to scholars and institutions who are likely to advocate preservation of a strong private sector." AEI scholar Michael Novak laid out similar arguments, and both men played a role in proselytizing this view in the corporate world, seeking to open up new funding sources for conservative policy institutions. At the same time, think tank entrepreneurs like Ed Feulner of Heritage and Edward Crane of CATO moved adroitly to cultivate corporate allies. At most conservative think tanks, corporate leaders now make up the overwhelming majority of board members. Even the American Enterprise Institute, among the most scholarly of conservative think tanks, has some two dozen corporate leaders on its board and only one academic, James Q. Wilson.

> *Conservative think tanks . . . can shape the national discussion on a given issue in a way that lobbyists cannot.*

The extent to which conservative think tanks rely on corporate funding support varies widely. The American Enterprise Institute and CEI have two of the highest levels of corporate support, with both getting roughly 40 percent of their 1996 revenues from corporations. CATO also received major corporate support, although it does not release the exact percentage of its revenue that comes from this source. In 1996, more than 100 corporations contributed to CATO, including Bell Atlantic, Exxon, Microsoft, Phillip Morris, Citicorp, Netscape, R.J. Reynolds, and General Motors. Substantial CATO money also comes from private businessmen.

The degree of direct quid pro quo that accompanies private sector giving to right-wing think tanks can be hard to document. At the most extreme end of the spectrum lies an organization like the Employment Policies Institute, which was started by a group of restaurant companies and gets most of its annual budget from corporate sources. EPI's sole purpose, it seems, is to produce studies opposing labor regulations, increases in the minimum wage, and other policies that benefit workers. Likewise, the American Legislative Exchange Council, which seek to shape state policies, is also largely a creature of the private sector—so much so that business leaders sit on all the committees that shape ALEC's policy work.

The Independent Institute appears to be somewhat more autonomous. Its funding comes from a range of corporations, foundations, and individuals. How beholden it is to a single one is hard to say. However, according to the *Times* article, Microsoft provided some 20 percent of the money that the Independent Institute raised during its last fiscal year, or over $200,000. In addition to the newspaper ads, Microsoft money helped pay for an Institute book that sought to systematically debunk the government's antitrust case.

Often, the link between the agenda of conservative think tanks and corporate interests is sporadic, tied to specific policies and projects. For example, in the mid-1990s, the Progress and Freedom Foundation, an institute closely tied to then–House Speaker Newt Gingrich, launched a major project on restructuring the Food and Drug Administration. Financing this work was at least $400,000 in contributions from drug, biotechnology, and medical-device companies. These companies have also given hundreds of thousands of dollars, perhaps millions, to a range of other right-wing groups that launched an unprecedented attack on the FDA during the 1990s.

Elsewhere, CATO's huge Social Security privatization project has been underwritten by $2 million or more in corporate money, much of it from financial service companies which would directly benefit from privatization. Hedging their bets, these same financial companies have paid for privatization work at nearly a half dozen other conservative think tanks as well. The campaign against the 1997 Kyoto global warming treaty waged by right-wing think tanks has been another area where corporate America has heavily invested in right-wing policy groups that advance its interest. The Competitive Enterprise Institute has been a particularly aggressive advocate of the notion that global warming is a "theory not a fact." Since 1991, CEI's budget has grown from less than $1 million to over $4 million.

Perhaps no conservative policy group works more closely with private industry than Citizens for a Sound Economy. With a board composed almost entirely of corporate leaders, and most of its funding coming from business, CSE is essentially a think tank and advocacy organization for corporate America, regularly tailoring its policy campaigns to suit the needs of its donors. The Koch family, which owns an energy conglomerate and has major interests at stake in Congress, is one of CSE's largest contributors, funeling as much as $1 million a year into CSE's coffers, both through Koch-controlled foundations and direct gifts. Contributions from numerous other corporations and industry groups have helped make CSE one of the fastest growing policy institutions in Washington. In 1996, CSE spent up to $5 million in a vigorous fight to roll back environmental legislation, concentrating fire on the EPA's Superfund, among other targets. More recently, CSE has joined the battle against the Kyoto treaty, helped lead the fight against the Microsoft anti-trust prosecution, and launched a number of other anti-regulatory campaigns in the areas of liability law, technology, and health care. Despite being funded almost exclusively by corporations, CSE has had surprising success at positioning itself as the grassroots voice of an antiregulatory American public.

For corporations, bankrolling conservative policy groups offers benefits not found in spending on lobbying or political contributions. Most of all, money spent on think tanks helps to buy respect for the self-interested positions of private companies. In public policy debates, scholarly experts and data-filled reports can legitimize certain viewpoints far more effectively than lobbyists. Also, while lobbyists typically focus on influencing the legislative process, conservative think tanks target their marketing efforts on many different audiences of "influentials," as well as the public at large. In this way they can shape the national discussion on a given issue in a way that lobbyists cannot. The Independent Institute's work defending Microsoft, for example, has clearly been designed to shape elite opinion.

Another advantage of funding conservative think tanks is that these institutions are able to advocate policy views that have not yet won acceptance within mainstream politics. Whereas many legislators will only embrace certain policy positions when it has become safe to do so, conservative policy institutions actively work to reframe the terms of political debate. In recent years, these institutions have helped push a number of previously fringe ideas—such as privatizing Social Security or abolishing the federal welfare entitlement—into the mainstream of political debate.

And the price tag for this policy work can't be beat. All corporate contributions to conservative think tanks have the advantage of being tax-deductible. While giving money to politicians is a direct non-deductible expense, giving money to AEI or Heritage—non-profits that must be non-partisan by law—confers the same tax benefits as donations made to the United Way.

Depending upon one's ideological outlook, the growing link between the private sector and public policy organizations can be seen as either wholly innocuous or decidedly ominous. Defenders of these ties, including David Theroux, president of the Independent Institute, argue that corporate donations don't affect the work of think tanks. "The academic process we use is independent of the sources of revenue," Theroux told the *Times*. Undoubtedly, there is much truth to this claim. Given their world view, Theroux and his colleagues at the Independent Institute would probably be bashing the government prosecutors after Microsoft regardless of who gave them money. Ed Crane, president of CATO, was a dedicated libertarian long before he turned that institute into a leading mouthpiece for corporate America's deregulatory agenda. In this view, the corporate underwriting of conservative think tanks is merely a happy marriage between free-marketeers and self-interested donors, just as Irving Kristol had originally proposed. It is, moreover, perfectly legal given current tax laws. Microsoft may have egg on its face after the revelations regarding the Independent Institute, but it won't be facing more charges from the Justice Department.

At the same time, something is clearly wrong with this situation. First, while these donations are indeed legal, they raise troubling questions about the intent of tax laws governing the non-profit sector. How is it that Microsoft gets the same tax deduction for funding advertising on its own behalf, via the Independent Institute, that it gets for donations to the arts or other charities? It seems unlikely that this is what Congress and the Treasury Department had in mind when it crafted the non-profit tax exemption earlier in this century. A rethinking of these statutes is long overdue.

Second, whatever the David Therouxs and Ed Cranes of the world may say, it is naive to imagine that conservative think tanks aren't extremely beholden to their funders in the business world or to the corporate leaders on their boards. This is simply the way that the power of the purse works. Just as politicians can't ignore the demands of major donors if they want to survive, neither can institutions ignore their benefactors. (Needless to say, this article was not submitted to Microsoft-owned *Slate* magazine.)

Finally, and somewhat ironically, the growing sophistication with which private funding of policy organizations can now be used to shape public debate raises major questions about the long-term effectiveness of campaign finance reform. Real campaign finance reform would largely dam not one, but two of the rivers of money flowing into America's politics. If big-time corporate giving to politicians was prohibited, the clout of private sector lobbyists would rapidly fade, since these lobbyists could no longer demand access and favors in return for campaign contributions. Deprived of more direct outlets, much corporate money intended to influence politics would probably be re-channeled into research and advocacy organizations, further boosting the size of the conservative policy colossus. Certainly this possibility should be taken into account by the liberal champions of campaign finance reform.

But whether campaign finance reform happens or not, there is an urgent need for better counterweights to the corporate propaganda machines that call themselves public policy research organizations. The familiar lament, of course, is that the money isn't out there to beef up mainstream and liberal public policy groups like the Economic Policy Institute or the Center for Budget and Policy Priorities. This is a myth. In truth, the philanthropic resources available on the left easily equal those on the right. The problem is that for the past two decades, liberal and mainstream foundations like Ford, Rockefeller, and MacArthur have seriously under-funded public policy work. Instead, they have put most of their money "on the street," seeking to effect change at the community level.

Meanwhile, the right gambled heavily on a top-down strategy aimed at dominating the elite national political discussion. This, it is now clear, was the superior game plan. Belatedly, foundations on the left may be learning from their historic blunder. More money is flowing to policy work, and several new progressive think tanks have been founded in recent years, including the New America Foundation and the Florence Fund (the sponsors of TomPaine.com) in Washington, D.C., and PolicyLink in Oakland, California. Still, the left remains years—and tens of millions of dollars—away from achieving anything close to parity in the war of well-funded ideas.

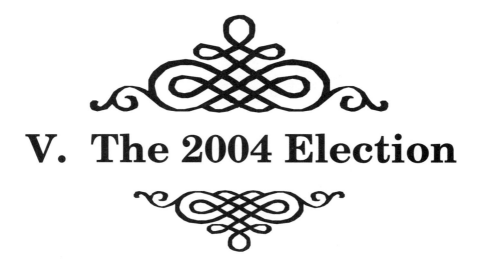

V. The 2004 Election

Editor's Introduction

Presidential and political historians have suggested that the 2004 presidential election may be one of the most important in U.S. history, with long-ranging implications for America's economy as well as its place in world affairs. There is also every indication that, like the 2000 election, this contest could be one of the closest ever as President George W. Bush fights off a spirited challenge from Senator John F. Kerry of Massachusetts.

In the four years since Bush took office, the world and the country have changed drastically. Terrorist attacks have fundamentally altered America's relationship with the outside world, while the subsequent War on Terror and the invasion of Iraq have further complicated the United States' role as a world power in the 21st century. Economically, the prosperity of the Clinton years gave way to recession, a downturn from which the nation has only fitfully recovered. Americans have more money in their pockets courtesy of President Bush's tax cuts, but the federal budget has in turn gone from a record surplus to a nearly half-trillion-dollar deficit, the largest ever. Consequently, there is much at stake in this election, and this chapter provides a glimpse into the factors and issues that will shape its outcome.

James Hilty places the 2004 race in perspective in a piece for *USA Today Magazine*. Written in March 2004, Hilty's article notes that President Bush and his Republican allies seem well positioned to claim victory in November, but Hilty predicts—correctly, as it turns out—that external events in Iraq and elsewhere were liable to change the dynamics of the race at any given moment. Then, "The Myths and Mysteries of Picking a No. 2" by David Greenberg for the *New York Times* details the various rationales that go into a candidate's selection of his vice presidential running mate. While at one time, a running mate was chosen for political balance, today, the emphasis is more likely to be on choosing an individual who can enhance a candidate's image.

The Hispanic vote is expected to be a deciding factor in 2004, Juan Gonzalez explains in an article for *Hispanic Business*. The fastest-growing segment of the American population, Hispanics have only just begun to exert their influence in the voting booth and will undoubtedly help reshape the nation's political landscape in the years to come.

The 2004 election is not just about the presidential race. Control of the House of Representatives and the Senate is up for grabs this year as well. Donald Lambro predicts in an article for the *Washington Times* that the Republicans are likely to maintain their hold on the Senate. Gregory L. Giroux similarly expects the Republicans to preserve their majority in the House, thanks in part to unprecedented congressional redistricting in Texas. However, both writers note, like Hilty in his essay, that the situation is relatively fluid and unexpected news could tilt the races either way. In the next selection, *Supreme Court Debates* explains the issue of congressional redistricting and how it could affect who controls the House in the years ahead.

Since its emergence in the 1990s, the Internet has played a greater role in American politics, both as a way to raise money and as a means to disseminate a candidate's message, as Ann M. Mack explains in her article for *Adweek*. However, how much of an impact do celebrity endorsements, long a staple of political campaigns, have on a candidate's election? J. Patrick Coolican tackles this question in a piece for *The Seattle Times*.

2004: An Election for the Ages?[1]

By James Hilty
USA Today Magazine, March 2004

The 2004 presidential election may prove of major historical importance, perhaps an election for the ages. Pres. George W. Bush has launched his reelection bid amid a flurry of international and domestic initiatives intended to consolidate the Republican hold on all levels of movement, smother his competition by preempting Democratic issues, and, ultimately, realign the American electorate and eliminate vestiges of Democratic rule. Seldom has a presidential election evoked such intense early discussion, much of it centered on one historical analogue. Rarely, too, has an incumbent been so focused on learning from the past. The question is: Can Bush avoid his father's fate?

Pres. George H. W. Bush's reelection defeat by Bill Clinton in 1992 proved that nothing in politics is certain. Flush with victory over Iraq in 1991, with his party trumpeting its role in bringing down the Berlin Wall and ending the Cold War, the elder Bush enjoyed spectacularly high approval ratings. Fighting the "wimp factor," maligning "this vision thing," while vaguely touting "a New World Order," Bush committed two fatal mistakes: appearing disinterested and disconnected from domestic concerns and miscalculating the splintering effects of H. Ross Perot's third-party candidacy. Clinton, admonished by advisor James Carville ("It's the economy, stupid"), campaigned relentlessly on national affairs and succeeded in reminding voters that Americans expect presidents to deliver more than military victories.

Now, 12 years later, Bush, transfixed by his father's failures, faces many of the same circumstances: another military victory over Iraq, high approval ratings, a stagnant economy, rising unemployment, huge Federal deficits, a health care system in disarray, cultural issues fanning rancorous elements among more conservative members in his party, and ratcheting partisan rhetoric. Yet, much else is different, and historical similarities before and after 1992 beckon attention.

Presidential election campaigns, once confined to nine or 10 months divided into the primary and general election seasons, have evolved into a perpetual process, commencing almost immediately after a presidential election and segmented into at least four distinct phases. The first phase of campaign 2004 concluded in the autumn of 2003 following congressional adjournment, the close of the Supreme Court session, and the President's African sojourn. By then, the issues for the upcoming election largely had been identified. Bush had established a record on which to stand for reelection. The Democratic challengers had declared themselves, prepared to move into the second stage, the primary season, to be followed by a respite (third stage) before the party conventions and the opening of the final, or general election, phase of the campaign.

Throughout the consolidation process, Bush, unlike his father at a similar point in 1991, forcefully asserted himself and successfully controlled the momentum and direction of national politics, with the clear intent of strengthening built-in advantages, holding the party base, attracting moderates, preempting Democrats, and gaining the political center. Through legislative initiatives and diplomatic strategies, he sought to rally the faithful and assuage the moderates' concerns, while minimizing potential openings for Democratic opponents and blocking dissenting Republican defections. While intently focused on avoiding the Republican mistakes of 1992, Bush and his advisors clearly have their eyes on a larger political objective: nothing less than an electoral realignment and virtual one-party control of government, further paving the way for the elimination of any remnants of 20th-century liberalism and its most offending domestic policy expressions in the Franklin Roosevelt and Lyndon Johnson presidencies.

> *The power of the presidency has magnified Bush's personality, campaign prowess, and political skills positively.*

Seldom has incumbency been so robustly and effectively leveraged. The power of the presidency has magnified Bush's personality, campaign prowess, and political skills positively. Arguing that he is a verbally challenged intellectual lightweight, Bush detractors questioned his competence and underestimated his political skills. He has proven remarkably effective on the stump, influencing the outcomes in several critical 2002 congressional races, and, time and again, ably maneuvering situations to his advantage and keeping the Democrats off guard.

As the polls reveal, the son is a much more partisan creature than the father. Under Bush's leadership, the Republican Party is waging two campaigns simultaneously: One (the high road, to project and defend the legitimacy of the presidency) will be taken by Bush himself, and a second (low road, to consolidate and expand GOP gains) is directed by Karl Rove and the Republican National Committee, using the full arsenal of political firepower. Bush's high road campaign includes both foreign and domestic objectives. To bolster his position among world leaders and regain lost credibility, he has expanded his personal participation in foreign affairs through hands-on involvement in seeking a resolution of the Arab-Israeli conflict, his victories in the UN Security Council on the reconstruction of Iraq, and his personal diplomatic sojourns to Poland, Russia, France, Africa, and Mexico.

To attract moderates' support, Bush has borrowed a page from Clinton's 1996 playbook. Just as Clinton co-opted Republicans by "ending welfare as we know it," balancing the budget, and placing more police on the streets, Bush temporarily abandoned party orthodoxy and co-opted opponents' issues by supporting tax credits for the working poor, orchestrating congressional compromises on prescription drug benefits through Medicare, and initiating a $15,000,000,000 program to combat AIDS globally. Meanwhile, Bush surrogates and Republican operatives are building a national political machine and exerting partisan pressures on an unprecedented scale, touching every corner of the country. Reapportionment battles in Texas and Colorado were coordinated by GOP leadership in Washington, led by Rove, who calls most of the political shots inside the White House, with controversial assistance from Attorney General John Ashcroft's Justice Department.

Inside the nation's capital, Republicans have taken dead aim on the Federal bureaucracy and the "regulatory state," which House Majority Leader Tom DeLay of Texas characterized as an unaccountable "leviathan that has run amok." Lobbyists also have come under fire from DeLay and Sen. Rick Santorum (R.-Pa.), who have demanded an end to the practice of lobbyists trying to maintain good relations with both parties. "If you play in our revolution," promises DeLay, "you have to live by our rules."

Democrats, according to a *New York Times*/CBS News survey, still enjoy a slight (33 to 30%) edge over Republicans in registered voters, and, as we know, in the 2000 election, more Americans combined preferred Al Gore and Ralph Nader to Bush. Just as in 1992, when Perot siphoned away votes from the elder Bush, Nader drew away enough voters from Gore to hand Bush his fragile, Court-anointed Electoral College victory. Changes occurring since 2001, however, have shifted the electoral calculus in Bush's favor. Congressional reapportionment will add Republican seats in the House and net Bush a gain of seven electoral votes in those states he carried in 2000. Additionally, the Republicans enjoyed substantial state and local gains in the 2002 elections, especially in the Sun Belt, which quickly is becoming the Republicans' version of the "Solid South." GOP gains in the Senate also are likely.

The Female Vote

Bush's advantage is bolstered by polls showing that voters strongly prefer Republicans in the area of national defense. Bush also benefits from one unexpected twist since Sept. 11. Women, who for several decades opposed Republican warmongering, have become more nervous than men about terrorism and national security. A Gallup survey noted a 21-point "fear gap" between the sexes. Moreover, 61% of the women surveyed in a Pew poll view the war in Iraq favorably. Although a majority of women still support Democrats on domestic issues (the economy, healthcare, prescription drug legislation, elderly benefits), a notable upswing has occurred in women's support for homeland security initiatives. As *U.S. News & World Report* editor Gloria Borger suggested, Bush may carry the soccer moms in 2004.

Bush's principal advantage emanates from his influence as wartime commander in chief, which under a doctrine of preemptive warfare against terrorism seems likely to continue indefinitely. As head of state, he is the star attraction of patriotic theatrics at ceremonies honoring national achievements. In 1992, the elder Bush played the patriotism card by celebrating the American flag, assailing those who would desecrate it, and virtually claiming the flag as a Republican campaign symbol. The younger Bush has gone his father one better, flying in on a combat jet and landing on the deck of a carrier to greet returning troops.

Meanwhile, the politics of terrorism have taken hold in America since 9/11. Similar to the Cold War mindset practiced until the fall of the Soviet Union, the questions have become: Which is the tougher party on terrorism? Whom do you find more credible in the

---

Bush appears to believe that most, if not all, economic problems can be solved with tax cuts.

---

war against terrorism? Do you feel safer today? The Administration has labored mightily to spin military victories in Afghanistan and Iraq as Republican accomplishments, achieved in spite of leftist protesters, French, German, Russian, and UN opposition, and scattered Democratic dissent. Bush skillfully has backed Democrats into a corner in which honest policy disputes come across as unpatriotic, or even "treason," as recklessly implied in attorney Anne Coulter's *Slander: Liberal Lies About the American Right*.

To assure reelection and avoid his father's fate, Bush must demonstrate the same verve on reinvigorating the economy as he has on national security. In the eyes of orthodox Republicans, George H. W. Bush's one unforgivable transgression was in breaking his promise not to increase taxes ("Read my lips . . ."): George W. Bush appears to have absorbed that lesson—to the point of obsession. Like the little boy with the hammer who thinks all things can be fixed with a little pounding, Bush appears to believe that most, if not all, economic problems can be solved with tax cuts.

In May, 2003, in accordance with a timetable set by the President, Congress passed a $350,000,000,000 tax cut, lowering rates and reducing taxes on dividends and capital gains. Sen. Mark Dayton (D.-Minn.) described the bill as a "shameful looting of the Treasury by the rich and powerful [to] line the pockets of the upper class." Republicans criticize, but do not refute, studies showing that by far the greatest benefits of the tax bill would go to the wealthy, who tend to have the most dividends and capital gains. Rep. Bill Thomas

(R.-Calif.), chairman of the House Ways and Means Committee, maintains this is playing the "class warfare card" and insists the Republican objective is to let American taxpayers keep their money.

In securing the tax cut, Bush exercised old-fashioned political muscle, enforcing Republican party loyalty before compromising in a timely manner. When House and Senate Republicans disagreed, Bush called them to the White House and "knocked heads." Appealing to party solidarity, he demanded adherence to his time-table and an end to squabbling over details. Bush dealt exclusively with Republicans and ignored Democrats' concerns. The GOP strategy is to extend indefinitely the temporary provisions of the 2003 bill to make it into a 1 trillion dollar tax cut package, rather than $350,000,000,000 as mandated. Bush will argue that opposition to permanent cuts is tantamount to supporting the largest tax increase in history. If the tax cuts harm rather than help the economy, no one is to blame but Bush and the Republicans.

"Republicans . . . had a hard time explaining why spending is bad, so they seized on the deficit as a proxy."—Bruce Bartlett, former Treasury official

---

Bush embarks on the campaign trail boasting two tax cuts at a time when government is amassing record deficits, thus signaling a dramatic and historic change in conservative thinking. Dating to the Ronald Reagan era, conservatives have attacked Democrats for running up deficits, which usually exacerbate inflation and raise interest rates, thus creating all sorts of difficulties. Perot's 1992 presidential campaign was predicated almost entirely on the issue of reducing Federal deficits, and House Speaker Newt Gingrich's 1994 "Contract with America" called for a Constitutional Amendment requiring a balanced budget. Now, rather suddenly, conservatives have decided that shortfalls no longer are evil. Bruce Bartlett, a Treasury official during the elder Bush's Administration, admits that Republicans' former zeal for balanced budgets was mainly a strategy for reducing government spending. "Republicans," he said, "had a hard time explaining why spending is bad, so they seized on the deficit as a proxy." Federal Reserve Chairman Alan Greenspan criticizes cutting taxes without offsetting spending reductions. Bush counters that the tax cuts will stimulate investment and promote economic growth, eventually erasing the deficit.

What Could Go Wrong?

Virtually all signs currently point towards sweeping Republican victories in 2004, but, as we learned in 1992, strange things can happen in presidential politics. Indeed, for all of the advantages gained since 9/11, Bush is vulnerable on a number of fronts. Domestically, the President's fixation on tax cuts to the detriment of other means of economic stimulation and job creation may, in the end, rebound to bite the Republicans where they sit. They can expect reverberations from shifting substantial burdens onto state and local governments and from extravagant run-ups in the Federal deficit at the same time government services are being cut. Slashing taxes on dividends and capital gains, moreover, signals to Americans that this Administration values investment over jobs by taxing work through payroll tariffs at a higher rate than dividends or capital gains. A falling dollar, increases in negative balance of payments, accelerating deficits, higher unemployment levels, and extended economic sluggishness could hand the Democrats many of the same advantages that Clinton enjoyed in 1992. By the same

---

"We've got a dictatorial president and a Justice Department that does not want Congress involved."—**Rep. Dan Burton**

---

logic, if the economy turns, unemployment declines, stock valuations increase, and productivity surges, Bush almost certainly is assured reelection.

Bush's greatest unspoken fear is that a moderate Republican will break away and, like Perot in 1992 and 1996, capture the center-right and moderate voters or that a Democratic centrist reinvigorates the issues successful for Clinton in 1992 and 1996 and that carried the popular vote for Gore in 2000. Bush betrays little concern about the future, however. Indeed, his regime conducts the affairs of state as though they enjoyed a 10,000,000-vote election majority—punishing enemies, purging the party, questioning the opposition's legitimacy—although fending off Democratic challengers and holding together diverse elements within his own party could grow more difficult as the next phases of the campaign unfold.

Claims of executive privilege, unparalleled exercises in the denial of civil liberties, and the use of secret, military tribunals to try citizens of other countries for threats against the U.S. have fostered suspicion and uncertainty, created a libertarian backlash, and even brought some steadfast Republicans to question the Administration and its motives. When, for example, Ashcroft invoked executive privilege to avert a congressional subpoena, Rep. Dan Burton (R.-Ind.), chairman of the House Committee on Government Reform, berated an Ashcroft aide, railing, "We've got a dictatorial president and a Justice Department that does not want Congress involved. . . . Your guy's acting like he's king."

Bush's attempts to gain the center without losing the right also have triggered stress points within the Cabinet. Prodded by senior political advisors, Bush dismissed his economic consultancy, led by Treasury Secretary Paul O'Neill, and accepted the resignations of Press Secretary Ari Fleischer and Environmental Protection Agency Director Christine Whitman.

To date, Bush has proved remarkably effective at maintaining party discipline. He has taken to the stump early and often, using the power and regalia of the presidency to resonate patriotic fervor and promote his policymaking. When Sens. Olympia Snowe (R.-Maine) and John Voinovich (R.-Ohio) blocked Bush's larger tax plan, insisting that the deficit could not tolerate a cut larger than $350,000,000,000, the President made a highly publicized visit to Ohio, apparently for the purpose of snubbing Voinovich in his own backyard and to make clear that he tolerates nothing less than full cooperation with his agenda. However, just as in 1992 when Patrick Buchanan challenged Bush's father, sparks from the "culture wars" could ignite simmering right wing resentments and bring them to the forefront of the 2004 campaign, and thus embolden and unify Bush critics. The elephant in the room, of course, is the right wing's principal objective of overturning *Roe v. Wade*. For that purpose, conservatives expect Bush to replace retiring Supreme Court justices with reliable conservatives.

The issue was rekindled in the summer of 2003 over the Court's bitterly argued 6–3 decision in *Lawrence v. Texas*, which declared the Texas Sodomy Law unconstitutional. Such a law, Justice Anthony Kennedy maintained, "demeans the lives of homosexual persons." Conservatives decried the "judicial activism" and "arrogance" of the Court. Santorum warned that striking down the Texas law opened the way to legalize adultery, bigamy, polygamy, incest, or, as he said, "the right to anything." Justice Antonin Scalia's dissent in *Lawrence* enjoined the issue. The decision, he declared, will create "a massive disruption of the current social order . . ." effectively decreeing "the end of all morals legislation." The Texas opinion, according to Scalia, is a clear signal "that the Court has taken sides in the culture war." It remains to be seen if Ralph Reed, former director of the Christian Coalition and now a White House operative, can hold the evangelical elements, preventing the fragile Bush coalition from imploding over the issue.

On the international front, Bush, unlike other wartime presidents, has declined the advice and guidance of the congressional opposition and brought no members of the Democratic party into prominent positions in his national security policy group. Franklin Roosevelt, by comparison, recruited two Republican stalwarts: Henry Stimson as Secretary of War and Frank Knox as Secretary of the Navy. Bill Clinton persuaded Sen. William Cohen (R.-Maine) to serve as Secretary of Defense. The Bush White House clearly intends that military victories in Afghanistan and Iraq translate into Republican/Bush victories. The downside of such partisan tactics is that the opposition is free to criticize when something goes wrong—and that it has.

Investigations into the *causus belli* for U.S. intervention in Iraq could prove embarrassing. No weapons of mass destruction have been found, so the Bush Administration's rationale for invading Iraq was without foundation. Conservatives and neoconservatives are satisfied, however, that the war ended a tyrannical regime, which in itself is sufficient justification. Bush's task will be to persuade the moderates and centrists as well.

The Administration also is vulnerable because of its astonishing lack of foresight in planning the post-war reconstruction of Iraq. During the second presidential debate in the 2000 election campaign, Bush criticized Clinton's policies in Somalia and the Balkans, stating, "I don't think our troops ought to be used for what's called nation-building." Forced to accept the necessity of such duties, Bush realizes that the longer U.S. involvement in Iraq continues and the more casualties mount, the more susceptible he is to Democratic criticism.

With all this said, one wonders if the fragmented, disarrayed Democrats are capable of coalescing to exploit Bush's weak points. For whatever reason, they lack the killer instinct and the stomach for demonizing opponents or turning elections into holy crusades. Democrats, however, may have no choice except to attack. And when they do, they must be prepared with not only questions, but some answers, or at least clear indications of what Democrats would have done differently.

The Myths and Mysteries of Picking a No. 2[2]

BY DAVID GREENBERG
THE NEW YORK TIMES, APRIL 11, 2004

Whom will Senator John F. Kerry pick as his running mate? John Edwards to compete in the South? Dick Gephardt to help in the Midwest? Bill Richardson to mobilize the Latino vote?

Most of the recent guesswork on the subject assumes that Mr. Kerry should use the choice to pick up a state or attract a constituency he couldn't win otherwise. But the idea that a running mate can deliver votes has always been dubious, and it's even less tenable today. Increasingly, candidates choose their understudies not for balance but to shape their image nationally.

A hundred years ago, most people voted for president strictly according to their party's line; having two regions or factions represented on the ticket made sense as a way to bolster party unity. But through the 20th century, power migrated from party bosses to the candidates. The nominee's image came to loom larger than his affiliation, and as a result the choice of running mate now matters mainly for what it says about the top contender himself.

Probably the worst-regarded choice of recent years was George H. W. Bush's selection of Dan Quayle in 1988. Vice President Bush, in his first major action as the presidential nominee, out from Ronald Reagan's shadow, seemed to use poor judgment in choosing an inexperienced candidate.

But the choice meant little, and Mr. Bush recovered. On the other hand, his rival, Gov. Michael S. Dukakis of Massachusetts, earned praise but few votes for his selection of Lloyd Bentsen, the moderate Texas senator—a choice made for the old-fashioned reasons of ideological and regional balance.

Conversely, the shrewdest choices have been those that enhanced the presidential nominee's image. Bill Clinton's selection of Al Gore in 1992 flouted the old wisdom about balance. By selecting another young, pragmatic Southerner, Mr. Clinton reinforced a central theme of his campaign—the need to discard both Republican and Democratic orthodoxies—while augmenting his image as a confident insurgent ushering in change.

In 2000, Mr. Gore followed the Clinton formula by picking Joseph I. Lieberman, the first Jew on a national ticket. That choice was hardly intended to help Mr. Gore in the Northeast, or with Jews, who already voted overwhelmingly Democratic. But it benefited Mr. Gore by casting him as willing to take bold steps.

Similarly, George W. Bush's choice of Dick Cheney didn't affect the election outcome in Wyoming, Mr. Cheney's home state. But it helped Mr. Bush turn his perceived lack of gravitas, a weakness, into a strength. The choice showed Mr. Bush as unafraid to turn to old hands for advice.

The idea of balancing a ticket started in the 19th century, when candidates owed their livelihoods to the party bosses who ran state and city machines—and whose ability to turn out voters decided elections. At convention time, the bosses had to maintain harmony within the party so they could rally the troops in the fall. They kept peace by allocating nominations regionally, calibrating their tickets with one Northeasterner, usually from New York, and one Midwesterner, usually from Ohio or Indiana. In the 15 elections from 1864 to 1920, two-thirds of the major party candidates came from those three states.

Progressive Era reformers, who viewed party politics as corrupt, weakened the bosses' power by instituting changes like primaries, which gave voters a voice in picking presidential nominees. Later, with television's arrival, candidates could reach voters directly, further marginalizing the bosses.

But as late as 1944, the bosses still held sway. In 1940, President Franklin D. Roosevelt had stiffed the bosses and selected Henry A. Wallace as his No.2. Four years later, however, the bosses, who considered Wallace a left-wing eccentric, struck back, replacing him with a respectable but nondescript Missouri senator, Harry S. Truman.

Still later, in 1952, it didn't even occur to Dwight D. Eisenhower, a political newcomer, to select his own understudy. When his adviser Herbert Brownell Jr. asked him his preference, he answered: "Gee, I don't know. I thought the convention handled that." Brownell polled Republican brokers, who liked Senator Richard M. Nixon.

When John F. Kennedy ran for president in 1960, he grasped that his own performance, not his running mate's home state, would be decisive. Nonetheless, he picked Lyndon B. Johnson, who he hoped (correctly) would carry Texas. Besides, conventional wisdom still held that a too-liberal ticket, especially on racial matters, would lose Southern votes. Indeed, for another generation the Democrats would often pair a Northerner with a Southerner to finesse conflicts on civil rights and related issues. The Republican Party similarly continued to offset a Rockefeller Republican with a staunch conservative, as with Ronald Reagan and George Bush in 1980.

By the 1980s, however, both parties had grown more ideologically uniform. Factionalism diminished, and with it the need for conciliatory gestures.

The final step was realizing that the choice of No. 2 provided a candidate with his first real chance to define himself. Reflecting the new calculus, in 1984 Walter F. Mondale decided on Geraldine A. Ferraro because, he said recently, he needed "a bold choice to change the political picture." Ms. Ferraro enlarged neither the ticket's geographic nor ideological appeal. What Mr. Mondale enhanced was his own image; his historic selection of a woman helped dispel—if briefly—perceptions that he was boring and meek. Mr. Clinton and others have operated in this vein.

Recent history suggests that it would be anachronistic for Mr. Kerry to try to capture a single state or find an ideological opposite in a vice president. His choice, rather, will have to give a corporeal reality to the themes and vision that he plans to advance.

Battleground '04[3]

BY JUAN GONZALEZ
HISPANIC BUSINESS, JANUARY/FEBRUARY 2004

For Republicans, the math is crystal clear: If President Bush wins the same percentage of the vote among every ethnic group this November that he received in 2000, he will lose the election by 3 million votes, according to a report by Republican pollster Matthew Dowd. And much of the increased Democratic margin could come from Hispanics, the fastest-growing sector of the electorate.

About 5.9 million Hispanics went to the polls in 2000, just 27 percent of the Hispanic voting-age population. But because of population growth, if the same percentage turns out this time, the number of Hispanic voters will exceed 6.7 million. Thus Mr. Bush would have to improve on the 35 percent of the Hispanic vote he received in 2000, while the Democratic candidate seeks to repeat the 62-percent share Democratic candidate Al Gore received.

The states with the biggest Hispanic populations—California, Texas, and New York—are considered safe in either the Republican or Democratic column, so the Hispanic vote will not be pivotal there. But in five "battleground" states—Florida, New Mexico, Arizona, Colorado, and Nevada—Hispanic voters will play a critical role. All but one of these states voted for Mr. Bush in 2000.

But the Hispanic vote has proven difficult to predict. "There is no Latino vote," says Fernando Oaxaca, a founder of the Republican Hispanic National Assembly. "You've got variations from region to region, from different nationalities, language preferences, [and] length of time in the U.S."

Yes, Cubans in South Florida routinely vote heavily Republican, while Puerto Ricans and Mexicans vote just as heavily Democratic. But the latter groups have been known to split their votes and provide significant spikes to mayoral Republican candidates such as Richard Riordan in Los Angeles and Rudy Giuliani and Michael Bloomberg in New York. And there is always the example of Ronald Reagan, who in his 1984 re-election campaign captured 42 percent of the national Hispanic vote.

Mr. Bush's policies toward Latin America and immigration make the 2004 Hispanic vote particularly difficult to predict. According to Democratic pollster Sergio Bendixen, a study last June showed 69 percent of Hispanics felt Mr. Bush had not kept his promise to make Latin America a top priority, and almost as many were unhappy about his failure to move forward with some sort of legalization for

---

undocumented immigrants. Of those who gave Mr. Bush negatives on these two issues, 60 percent said they plan to vote for a Democrat for president, while only 24 percent said they would vote for Mr. Bush. With Mr. Bush's announcement of an ambitious new temporary worker program, those numbers are likely to shift in the coming months.

John Zogby, CEO of bipartisan polling firm Zogby International, says that Mr. Bush's approach to Latin America could still hurt him if the Democrats highlight the issue. "Given the close elections we're having nationally, we are not talking about moving tens of millions of voters in one direction or another," Mr. Zogby says. "Moving a few thousand voters can decide an election."

Other experts warn that equating the Hispanic vote with immigration issues is a mistake because most Hispanic voters are U.S. born. "Education, the economy, safety in the neighborhoods is the main concern for Latinos," says Harry Pachon of the Tomas Rivera Policy Institute.

"Education, the economy, safety in the neighborhoods is the main concern for Latinos."—**Harry Pachon, Tomas Rivera Policy Institute**

But perhaps more important than defining key issues will be turning out the vote in those five battleground states. Florida ranks as the biggest prize, but the Hispanic vote there no longer fits political molds. The 2000 Census confirmed that Florida has become the fastest-growing state for Puerto Ricans: More than 500,000 boricuas, many of them retired New Yorkers, now reside along an east-west corridor centering on Orlando. The state also has growing Dominican, Colombian, and Nicaraguan populations. When Mel Martinez resigned as HUD secretary to run for the Republican nomination for a U.S. Senate seat in Florida, Republican strategists were aware that his political base is in central Florida.

In New Mexico much has changed in the four years since the state delivered a razor-thin margin of victory to Mr. Gore. Former Clinton cabinet member Bill Richardson is now governor, and a popular elected official even among some Republicans. The appointed chair of the Democratic National Convention, Mr. Richardson wants to exert a major impact on this race. He engineered the first Hispanic-oriented presidential Democratic debate there, and he has established a $4 million nonprofit fund, Moving America Forward, to mobilize Hispanic voters in New Mexico and three of the other battleground states.

"Bill wants to run for president in 2008," says a top Democratic leader. "And he's made no secret of wanting to be considered as a vice-presidential running mate this year."

> *5.5 million Hispanic citizens of voting age remain unregistered.*

But dwarfing Mr. Richardson's effort is the $55-million voter education and mobilization operation put together by New York union leader Dennis Rivera. While normally seen as a labor leader (he sits on the AFL-CIO executive committee) the Puerto Rico–born Mr. Rivera is even more influential among Hispanic politicians than he is in organized labor. For this election, he has developed a novel strategy called "Bush Bucks." As part of the campaign, he has earmarked $35 million from his union's war chest to dispatch 1,000 organizers outside of New York to work full-time in the battleground states to defeat Mr. Bush.

In addition, Mr. Rivera and Democratic National Committee member Bill Lynch have joined Carl Pope of the Sierra Club to create yet another voter registration group. The organization already has raised more than $20 million to target "marginalized" populations. Given that at least 5.5 million Hispanic citizens of voting age remain unregistered, Mr. Rivera believes a massive campaign to reach even a portion of that population in states such as New Mexico and Arizona could produce unexpected results.

Arizona is a state that Bill Clinton won in 1996, but Mr. Gore lost in 2000 by less than 100,000 votes. The state is 25 percent Hispanic and in the last four years has elected a Democratic woman governor and added another Hispanic congressman, Raul Grijalva. More than half of its population growth since 2000 has been Hispanic.

"It's nasty there because of the border and immigration question," says Mr. Oaxaca. "You may have some anti-Republican backlash among Hispanics because of those attacks on immigrants at the border."

In Nevada, Mr. Bush won by less than 22,000 votes in 2000. But the state's Hispanic segment nearly doubled between 1990 and 2000, to almost 20 percent of the population, and many of those Hispanics are highly organized through unions in the hotel and gaming industries.

As for Colorado, Mr. Bush won the state's vote with 51 percent in 2000, but his environmental policies have hurt him there. That development, coupled with the growth of Colorado's Hispanic population, points to a much closer presidential vote this year.

With Republicans expected to raise record amounts of money for this year's campaign, they should flood Spanish-language media with advertising, as they did in 2000 in Florida and other states in an effort to get out their message. Meanwhile, Democrats will spend the first few months of the year battling over their nomination.

So far none of the Democratic candidates has attracted much support in the Hispanic community, although Howard Dean has the largest list of Hispanic supporters including Arizona's Mr. Grijalva, union leader Mr. Rivera, and members of Congress Robert Menendez (New Jersey), Nydia Velazquez (New York), and Loretta Sanchez and Lucille Roybal Allard (California).

Dick Gephardt carries the backing of Arizona Congressman Ed Pastor. John Kerry has support from former Clinton appointees Henry Cisneros and Aida Alvarez. And Al Sharpton of New York has support from Congressman Jose Serrano and former Bronx Democratic Party Chief Roberto Ramirez.

Whatever the outcome in November, the Hispanic vote will play a larger role than ever, and it will be complex and unpredictable.

Women Voters Key in 2004 Presidential Election[4]

By Darlisa Y. Crawford
USINFO.STATE.GOV, April 14, 2004

An eligible woman voter is more likely to cast a ballot in the next presidential election than her male counterpart if a pattern identified in the 2000 election continues. According to the U.S. Census Bureau, 61 percent of eligible women voters cast a ballot in the 2000 presidential election. That level of participation is higher than the 58 percent of eligible males who voted.

The "Gender Gap"

In the 1960s American women were more likely to identify with the Republican Party than the Democratic Party. Richard Nixon narrowly carried the women's vote in 1960 after the first televised debate against Kennedy. Political analyst Rachel Alexander concluded that for the first time voters evaluated a presidential candidate's performance on television, which influenced how voters cast their ballots. By the 1980 election between Reagan and Carter, this partiality toward the Republican Party had changed. Carter won the women's vote.

The Gallup Organization, a major independent polling firm, concludes that in every presidential election since 1980 a gender gap has existed. Women have more often supported Democratic candidates while men have more often supported Republican candidates. In presidential elections the gap has ranged from 4 percent to 11 percent. In 1992 women voters supported Clinton in larger numbers than men by 4 percent. In the 2000 election, Al Gore won the women's vote by 11 percent.

Recent Gallup polls report that Republican incumbent President George W. Bush has received higher job approval ratings from men than from women in all but three polls conducted since he took office more than three years ago. In 2004, men have given Bush a job approval rating that is seven points higher than women have given him. Ballot tests this year also show that Bush receives greater support in his bid for re-election among men than among women, according to the Gallup Organization.

---

4. Article by Darlisa Y. Crawford from *usinfo.state.gov*, the official Web site of the United States Department of State.

"Security Moms"

On the other hand, women support the war on terrorism and military spending at the same level as men, according to recent polls. Some political analysts attribute the narrowed gender gap to the September 11 terrorist attacks. They suggest that women who have been reticent to support the use of military force now view it as essential for the protection of their families and communities. Women's support for higher defense budgets increased to 47 percent in October 2001 from 24 percent earlier in the year. The swing voters referred to as "soccer moms" of 2000 may be replaced with "security moms" in 2004.

According to the Pew Research Center for the People and the Press, women's support for military spending remains at levels much higher now. "There is no gender gap on this point, because people are united behind the president," says Linda Divall, a Republican pollster.

An important disparity exists between married women voters and unmarried women voters.

The Single Vote

An important disparity exists between married women voters and unmarried women voters. Women of voting age who have never been married, divorced, or widowed comprise 42 percent of all registered women voters. In the 2000 presidential election, unmarried women voters represented the same percentage of the electorate as Jewish, African American, and Latino voters combined. For this group, the highest priority issues are health care, employment, education, job security, and retirement benefits. Over 21 million unmarried women voters never cast a ballot on election day, according to data from Women's Voices. Women Vote., a nonprofit organization dedicated to increasing women's voter registration.

"We have to help these women understand they can absolutely determine the outcome of the election," says Christina Desser, cofounder of the organization.

In the 2002 mid-term elections, 56 percent of married women voted for Republican Party candidates, compared to 39 percent of unmarried women. Harvard University assistant professor of public policy Anna Greenberg associates "moral traditionalism" that appeals to married women with the Republican Party.

Campaigning for the Women's Vote

Women's concerns will be important topics of debate on the campaign trail this election season. The Republican National Committee has launched a program called Winning Women, designed to recruit and train female Republican candidates for public office and to reach out to female voters. The Democratic National Committee has created the DNC Women's Vote Center that educates and mobilizes women voters about electing Democratic candidates for public office.

Both Massachusetts Senator John Kerry and President Bush have emphasized issues that resonate with women—job creation, healthcare, and education—in recent campaign speeches. First Lady Laura Bush features prominently in her husband's re-election advertisements. Kerry's daughters, Alexandra and Vanessa, promote their father's concerns with jobs and the environment on the campaign trail.

"The women's vote will decide the next election, as it has since 1980," stated political psychologist Dr. Martha Burke. "Candidates have an opportunity to showcase their views on the issues women care most about—violence, the pay gap, education, and economic security. Those who address women's concerns directly are likely to strike a chord."

Republicans Seen Retaining Control of Senate[5]

By Donald Lambro
The Washington Times, April 28, 2004

Democrats have new opportunities to pick up Senate seats this year, but the Republicans are still favored to make net gains in the South, where President Bush and his party draw their strongest support.

Entering 2004, Republicans appeared to have a slam-dunk shot at strengthening their tenuous 51-seat hold on the Senate with a bonanza of five open Democratic seats in Florida, Georgia, Louisiana, North Carolina, and South Carolina. But their lopsided Southern advantage has been offset to some degree by unexpected Republican retirements in Colorado and Oklahoma that have enlarged the Democrats' targeted-for-takeover list.

Even so, veteran congressional campaign trackers say they think Republicans will keep control of the Senate in November and add a seat or two to their slim majority, although the battle for political dominance in the chamber has clearly tightened in recent weeks.

"Our money is still on Republican retention of the Senate and certainly the House, but as Lewis Carroll's Alice observed in Wonderland, things are getting 'curiouser and curiouser,'" writes Charlie Cook in his latest *Cook Election Preview*.

Stuart Rothenberg in his monthly *Rothenberg Political Report* said Democrats' chances of taking control of the Senate have improved, but he predicts either "no net change or a GOP gain of a seat."

Although Democratic Senate prospects have improved, "they still have a more difficult road ahead than do the Republicans. They need to win seven of the 10 most competitive Senate races to get to 50 seats and eight to get to 51, which they would need if Bush wins re-election," Mr. Rothenberg said.

Of the eight targeted open races, Mr. Rothenberg sees two Democratic seats—in Georgia and South Carolina—leaning toward Republican takeovers and only one Republican seat, held by retiring Illinois Sen. Peter G. Fitzgerald, falling to the Democrats.

All the rest, plus the seats of Republican Sen. Lisa Murkowski of Alaska and Democratic Sen. Tom Daschle of South Dakota, are rated competitive, although Republicans have a slight mathematical edge. Four Democratic seats in Florida, Louisiana, North Caro-

---

lina, and South Dakota are "tossups," he says, but only three Republican seats fall into that category: Alaska, Colorado, and Oklahoma.

But that's not the way that the Democratic Senatorial Campaign Committee [DSCC] sees things.

"The Democrats have had one of the best recruiting classes in quite awhile, while Republicans have clearly failed to recruit top-tier candidates from Washington state to California," says DSCC spokesman Cara Morris. "If the elections were held today, public polling shows the Democrats would be at 52 seats."

Among the five open Senate Democratic contests in the South:

- Georgia: Several Republicans are vying for the seat of retiring Sen. Zell Miller, a conservative Democrat who is campaigning for Mr. Bush. Rep. Johnny Isakson is the front-runner in a field of Republican candidates that includes Rep. Mac Collins and businessmen Al Bartell and Herman Cain, chief executive officer of Godfather's Pizza. Rep. Denise L. Majette and businessman Cliff Oxford are seeking the Democratic nod. Most analysts see this as the Republicans' strongest race and a likely pickup.

- Florida: Former Housing and Urban Development Secretary Mel Martinez, with strong White House backing, faces former Rep. Bill McCollum, who lost a Senate bid in 2000. Early polls show Mr. McCollum leading a crowded field that includes four other Republican candidates. Three Democrats battling to succeed retiring Sen. Bob Graham include Rep. Peter Deutsch, Miami-Dade Mayor Alex Penelas and former state Education Commissioner Betty Castor, the party's front-runner.

- South Carolina: Another multicandidate Republican primary field complicates the party's efforts to pick up retiring Democratic Sen. Ernest F. Hollings' seat: Rep. Jim DeMint, former state Attorney General Charles Condon, real-estate developer Thomas Ravenel and former Gov. David Beasley. Democrats have united behind state Superintendent of Education Inez Tenenbaum, but South Carolina is one of the most Republican states in the country "and any Democrat in a federal race has plenty of obstacles to overcome if Republicans unite," Mr. Rothenberg says.

- North Carolina: The race is between Erskine Bowles, President Clinton's former chief of staff who lost a 2002 Senate bid against Elizabeth Dole, and Rep. Richard M. Burr, a five-term congressman who won re-election in 2002 with 70 percent of the vote. Polls give Mr. Bowles, who has raised $3.3 million, the edge, but observers say the race for former Democratic presidential candidate Sen. John Edwards' seat is a tossup.

- Louisiana: The field of candidates vying for Sen. John B. Breaux's seat suggests that this race might be settled in an end-of-the-year runoff under the state's open-primary system. Republican Rep. David Vitter leads in the polls, but former Gov. Buddy Roemer, also a Republican, might enter the race. On the Democratic side are Rep. Chris John, state Treasurer John Kennedy and state Rep. Arthur Morrell.

Daunting Task of Takeover[6]

BY GREGORY L. GIROUX
CQ WEEKLY, AUGUST 9, 2003

There is little doubt that the 2004 congressional elections will be influenced by broad factors such as the strength of the economy, President Bush's re-election fortunes, and the state of the war against terrorism.

But the next campaign for control of the House is not shaping up to be a "macro" contest, in which those national trends primarily determine the outcome. Instead, which party runs the House in the 109th Congress will probably be determined on the "micro" level— the aggregate of the elections in each of the 435 congressional districts. And that poses a monumental challenge for the Democrats, who will be seeking to retake control of the chamber after a decade in the minority.

Democrats need a wide playing field of politically competitive districts if they hope to gain the 12 seats required to take the majority from the Republicans, who now hold 229 seats, to 205 for the Democrats and 1 for an independent who sides with the Democrats. That is a tall order in an era when most incumbents are "safe"—and made safer by redistricting in 2001 and 2002 that narrowed the universe of competitive races.

The structural advantage Republicans enjoy in the 2004 House campaign can be gleaned from the following statistics: Although he won the presidency in the Electoral College, Bush took only 47.9 percent of the popular vote, which Democrat Al Gore won by 540,000 votes. Nonetheless, under the congressional maps that now are in place, Bush carried 237 of the 435 districts—or 54 percent of all the House seats that will be contested next year.

That is in part the result of continued population growth in the South and the West, areas largely favorable to Republicans; the reapportionment following the 2000 census shifted seats mainly to those regions. And the GOP's edge also is in part the result of partisan redistricting plans that Republicans succeeded in enacting prior to the 2002 elections in states where they controlled the process— including such population centers as Florida, Pennsylvania, Michigan, and Ohio.

The GOP is seeking to press its advantage even further by pushing—against emphatic resistance from the Democrats—to redraw the House map in Bush's home state of Texas, where Democrats

---

now hold a 17-15 advantage in the delegation under a map invoked by a court panel. A special session of the state Legislature is deadlocked on the issue, but Republicans have vowed not to give up.

Democratic leaders acknowledge that they will need some sort of national political "wind" to form at their backs if they are to be propelled to the majority in 15 months. Since 1982, when the party picked up a net of

> *"The great majority of Republican seats are safe."*—John J. Pitney Jr., political scientist

26 seats, its biggest gains have been nine seats in both 1990 and 1996—short of their 2004 target of 12.

Democratic strategists insist that their prospects have improved in recent months. They say they have candidates who are very interested in running; that Bush's popularity has declined, reducing the likelihood that he will have "coattails" for his fellow Republicans; and that voters are raising questions about the Republicans' stewardship of the economy.

"There's a breeze behind us now, and I think that is helping us," said Robert T. Matsui of California, chairman of the Democratic Congressional Campaign Committee (DCCC).

But a big question is whether Democrats can muster the resources and recruit strong candidates in enough districts to overcome the GOP advantage.

"There are only a limited number of takeover targets," said John J. Pitney Jr., a political scientist at Claremont McKenna College. "The great majority of Republican seats are safe."

GOP's to Win or Lose

But Republicans cannot afford overconfidence. They will be pressed to make the case to voters for continued GOP control of the federal government.

The Republicans controlled both halves of Congress as well as the White House during the first five months of 2001, but the Senate flipped to the Democrats that June after Vermont's James M. Jeffords quit the GOP.

So the 108th Congress is the first sustained period in which the Republicans have controlled the Senate, the House, and the presidency at the same time since the 83rd Congress of 1953 and 1954. And unlike in 2002—when they were able to run against the Democratic-run Senate as an obstacle to progress—the Republicans must stand on their own record this time.

"2004 is very much going to be a referendum on us," said Thomas M. Davis III of Virginia, the previous chairman of the National Republican Congressional Committee (NRCC). "You'll find that when one party controls the presidency, the House, and the Senate, these are referendums on the incumbents."

Davis said that he is counseling House Republicans to ignore Democratic strategy and concentrate instead on priorities such as conducting the war against terrorism, boosting the economy, and enacting a prescription drug plan. "Whatever the Democrats do is irrelevant," Davis said. "It's really what we do, what we're able to pass and how we're able to frame things."

> *"A bad economy is always an opportunity for the 'out' party."*—**John J. Pitney Jr., political scientist**

Republicans and independent analysts agree that Democrats stand to benefit if the economy worsens, given that the GOP is the party in charge.

"The economy remains a national problem and a Democratic opportunity," Pitney said. "A bad economy is always an opportunity for the 'out' party, especially the Democrats."

But the Democratic Party's own financial hardship—a shortage of campaign cash—may undercut its efforts to convince voters that it would be the better steward of the economy. In the first six months of this year, the NRCC reported raising more than three times as much as the DCCC—$45.5 million to $14.5 million.

Playing Under New Rules

The Democrats had been more competitive in fundraising when the parties were allowed to collect and spend unregulated "soft money," but those were exactly the kind of donations that were banned by the campaign finance law (PL 107-155) that took effect for this election cycle.

Thomas M. Reynolds of New York, who succeeded Davis as NRCC chairman, expressed skepticism that Democrats would be capable of producing more competitive challengers in 2004 than they did in 2002, when they benefited from soft money.

Democrats argue that they will have adequate resources to get their message out. And they say the key fundraising statistic is cash on hand. Because the DCCC had spent far less, it had nearly as much of a reserve ($6.4 million) as the NRCC ($6.6 million) at the end of June, when the organizations made their most recent filings to the Federal Election Commission. However, the DCCC also was carrying $2.7 million in debt, while the NRCC was debt-free.

Without soft money to rely upon, the House campaign organization is turning to incumbents who are politically safe and who can part with some of their huge campaign treasuries in the form of smaller "hard money" contributions.

Well-financed incumbents have also steered money to the campaign committees of more vulnerable members. The GOP has held two Retain Our Majority Program (ROMP) events that boosted the campaign treasuries of 20 lawmakers from competitive districts. The DCCC has identified 18 Democrats who are most in need of campaign cash.

It is unclear how many "open seats"—which tend to be more competitive than districts defended by incumbents—will emerge in 2004. At this early stage, there have been few announced departures, and most of them are in solidly partisan districts.

One exception to that rule is Pennsylvania's 15th District, which three-term Republican Patrick J. Toomey is leaving open to challenge the renomination of GOP Sen. Arlen Specter. The district, which includes the Lehigh Valley cities of Allentown and Bethlehem, could be a bellwether of the 2004 campaign. Republicans, having already recruited a strong candidate in state Sen. Charles Dent, might have an early edge. But the district's voters preferred Gore in 2000; it was represented from 1993 to 1999 by Democratic moderate Paul McHale and could swing back to that party in tough economic times.

Shaky Seats Targeted

Recognizing the difficulty in dislodging veteran incumbents, Democratic strategists are focusing heavily on members of the Republican freshman class who represent politically competitive districts.

The most vulnerable among them may be Max Burns of Georgia's 12th District. He won by 10 percentage points in 2002, even though the district along the state's eastern edge had been drawn by the Democratic-controlled General Assembly to elect a Democrat. Voters there favored Gore by 10 points, and Democrats describe Burns' win as an aberration; their nominee, businessman Charles Walker Jr., was hobbled by revelations of past arrests. So far, two Democrats are seeking the nomination to challenge Burns: Athens-Clarke County Commissioner John Barrow and state Sen. Doug Haines. Barrow has jumped out to an early lead in fundraising, posting $272,000 in overall receipts.

Georgia Democrats also are aiming to take on another upset Republican winner from last year: Phil Gingrey of the northwestern 11th District. He raised $846,000 in the first half of this year, more than any other House freshman.

Democratic strategists are eyeing Arizona's 1st District, a vast, rural expanse in the northeastern part of the state that has a large percentage of veterans and American Indians. Republican Rick Renzi won by 4 points in 2002 over Democrat George Cordova, a politically inexperienced businessman.

Cordova is seeking a rematch. But also trying for comebacks are three of his top 2002 primary opponents: Steve Udall, a former county attorney and a cousin of Colorado Democratic Rep. Mark Udall and New Mexico Democratic Rep. Tom Udall; attorney Diane Prescott; and Fred DuVal, a former Clinton administration official, who finished fourth. Paul Babbitt, a county supervisor and brother of former Gov. Bruce Babbitt, also is looking at the race.

As the winner of the closest House election in 2002, Republican Bob Beauprez would be expected to face fierce Democratic opposition in Colorado's 7th District, in the Denver suburbs. But the Republican-controlled Legislature altered the state's congressional map to give Beauprez more GOP voters. That map faces a legal challenge from Democrats, though. If the new lines are overturned, Beauprez could face a vigorous challenge in 2004.

The Democrats are not only targeting newcomers. High on their hit list is Republican John Hostettler, who has won five close races in southern Indiana's 8th District. Hostettler, who largely shuns the fundraising circuit, raised just $1,100 in the second quarter of this year. Democrat Jon Jennings, a former assistant coach for the Boston Celtics, is making a bid.

Party strategists also are eyeing districts in which Democratic statewide candidates traditionally have done well. These include eastern Alabama's 3rd, held by freshman Michael D. Rogers; eastern Connecticut's 2nd, represented by two-term Republican Rob Simmons; and Kentucky's Louisville-based 3rd, where Anne M. Northup has won a quartet of nail-biter victories.

In other potentially competitive districts, Democratic strategists say they expect to field more competitive challengers to Republicans than they did in 2002. These include northwestern Missouri's 6th, held for two terms by Sam Graves; central New Jersey's 7th, held for two terms by Mike Ferguson; and Pennsylvania's 18th in the Pittsburgh area, represented by freshman Tim Murphy.

Democratic-Held Seats

Already in the majority, Republican strategists will emphasize protection of the seats they hold. But they have no intention of playing only defense. The GOP is targeting conservative and moderate Democrats who represent districts that voted strongly for Bush in the 2000 presidential election.

In several districts, Republican challengers who narrowly lost last year are back for a second try.

In northern Kentucky's 4th District, businessman Geoff Davis has been laying the groundwork for a rematch with Ken Lucas, one of the most conservative House Democrats. Former state Rep. John Swallow is bidding for another shot at Democrat Jim Matheson, who won a second term in Utah's sprawling 2nd District by less than 1 percentage point in 2002. Pilot Adam Taff is gunning for another go-round with Democrat Dennis Moore, who has held Kansas' suburban 3rd District since 1999. But Davis, Swallow, and Taff are likely to face primary opposition.

Republican officials are not waiting for the theatrical battle over redistricting to run its course in Texas. They are weighing serious challenges to two veteran Democrats in mainly rural districts that are expected to overwhelmingly favor Bush's re-election: Charles W. Stenholm of the 17th District and Chet Edwards of the 11th. GOP strategists are also looking at the 4th District, east of Dallas, held by Democrat Ralph M. Hall, who at 80 is the House's oldest member and may not seek a 13th term.

Redistricting Battles

Partisan Reapportionment of Congressional Maps[7]

SUPREME COURT DEBATES, FEBRUARY 2004

Following the decennial census in 2000, State legislatures began their constitutional duty to draw new congressional districts to take into account population changes.

In several States, there were vocal complaints that partisan legislatures had designed maps that were contorted and drawn purely to maximize political benefit for the majority party.

Anger surrounding the partisan drawing of congressional maps is not a new phenomenon, however. The term that describes such a practice, "gerrymandering," dates back to 1812, and State legislatures have long attempted to craft maps that tilt the playing field toward the drawing party.

A recent development, however, is the creation of advanced statistical computer models that allow politicians to scientifically draft congressional maps that maximize political advantage. In a process called "cracking and packing," a map can be designed to break opposing party stronghold areas into different districts to dilute their power (cracking) or group a party's voters into a single district, leaving fewer in the remaining districts (packing).

The U.S. Supreme Court has been far from silent on the issue of congressional redistricting, although it has addressed political gerrymandering only once. A majority of the Court's cases have focused on the consideration of race in the drawing of maps (including the *Shaw v. Reno* (1993) line of cases) and one-person–one-vote cases such as *Reynolds v. Sims* (1964), which required minimal population deviations among districts.

In *Davis v. Bandemer* (1986), the U.S. Supreme Court denied a challenge to an Indiana legislative district map on the grounds that it was partisan gerrymandering—but a majority of the justices left open the possibility that a State legislature could go too far in designing a map for purely political gain.

With this decision in mind, a group of Pennsylvania Democratic voters sued their State, alleging that the new map was an unconstitutional violation of their political rights.

---

7. Article from *Supreme Court Debates,* February 2004. Copyright © *Congressional Digest.* Reprinted with permission.

Although the Democratic voters won an early court battle, a Federal district court later upheld a redesigned map—ruling that it was not unconstitutionally partisan. The voters appealed to the U.S. Supreme Court, which granted certiorari on June 27, 2003, and heard arguments on December 10.

Before the Court, lawyers for the Appellant Democratic voters argued that the Pennsylvania map was dangerous to democracy. It shut some voters out of the political process by preventing them from electing candidates from their party, ensured that incumbents would be even more likely to get reelected, and increased the likelihood that partisan extremists would win in politically lopsided districts.

Bandemer held that partisan gerrymandering can go too far, the lawyers continued, and if this case didn't reach that point, none ever would. The U.S. Constitution limits a State's discretion when it creates new district maps. They concluded by detailing a series of tests based on Court precedent that could be used to identify unconstitutional district mapping—such as whether a party could win a majority of congressional seats in a State without their getting a majority of the total votes.

For a congressional map to be unconstitutional, the appellants would have to prove they were denied a voice in the political process.

Lawyers for Pennsylvania responded that the *Bandemer* standard was much more stringent than the Appellants were claiming. For a congressional map to be unconstitutional, the appellants would have to prove they were denied a voice in the political process—and simply having their district represented by a member of a different party is not enough. They also argued that political orientation does not qualify them as a disadvantaged group. A person's political preferences, unlike race, can change at any time. And oftentimes, individuals registered with one party vote for another party's candidate.

As for the argument that political gerrymandering fosters extremism, the State lawyers countered that by that logic, the U.S. Senate would be free from the partisan rancor present in the House—which was clearly not the case.

In the end, they concluded, any problems arising from partisan maps were self-correcting. People move, voting patterns change, and the influence of political parties ebbs and flows. In 10 years, Democrats might have regained control of the Pennsylvania Legislature and could then redraw maps to their liking.

With redistricting battles currently being waged in courts in Texas and Colorado, *Vieth*, et al. *v. Jubilirer*, et al. could have an immediate impact on congressional races around the country. In the long run, the Court's decision will be closely studied as State legislatures prepare to redraw once again congressional district lines following the 2010 census.

How the Internet Is Changing Politics[8]

By Ann M. Mack
Adweek, January 26, 2004

Old Glory sways limply in the breeze from a hardware store just west of The Grand Saloon, an old-school pub on East 23rd Street in Manhattan whose red neon sign and copper facade promise an inviting retreat from the biting January wind. Inside, about 100 Wesley Clark supporters strain to hear a blonde-bobbed, middle-aged woman with a slight voice.

"We can't hear you," one of them shouts. "Can you speak up?" pleads another, cupping his hand to his ear.

A stout, white-haired veteran takes a swig of dark beer and swaps military credentials with an older man who wears a "Veterans for Clark" pin. A curly-haired, fortysomething woman admires a fellow supporter's regalia, which includes a button that reads, "Women for Clark," and another that relays an endorsement from hip-hop group OutKast. "Where did you get those?" she asks. The reply: "I found them on eBay."

It's the first Monday of the new year, and Clark, the former U.S. Army general and NATO commander, knows where to find his troops. Some 57,000 supporters have registered to attend monthly meetings at hundreds of establishments like this one nationwide. They come from all walks of life, but many of them have one key thing in common: They got here via the Internet.

Where political campaigning is concerned, the Web is no longer only a place to troll for rare buttons. It is no longer a newfangled top-down communications tool. Increasingly, politicians and their advisers are realizing the true potential for galvanizing their campaigns online. They are beginning to understand the Web—and, to some extent, harness it—as a fundraising, organizing, community-building, marketing, and get-out-the-vote mechanism.

Much of this is due to Sen. John McCain, R-Ariz. The first presidential candidate to fully harness the power of the Internet, McCain orchestrated a huge online fundraising blitz after his upset victory in the 2000 New Hampshire primary. In this campaign season, it is Howard Dean who has taken the McCain lesson to heart. The former Vermont governor's team, led by campaign manager and

---

Internet evangelist Joe Trippi, leveraged the Web to build grass-roots support and catapult the one-time longshot into one of the top contenders in the race for the Democratic nomination.

"Howard Dean, a nobody from nowhere with no chance, used the Internet basically in the course of seven months to become the leading candidate of the Democratic Party for president," says Phil Noble, founder of Politics Online, a Charleston, S.C., firm that provides tools for online campaigning and fundraising.

Dean's disappointing showing in the Iowa caucuses raises doubts about his Internet-driven campaign's ability to bring in the votes. Still, it seems clear that many of Dean's methods for raising awareness, support, and funds online will be emulated—and already have been, to some degree, by his rivals in this race.

Dean's strategy has been propelled largely by the activist nature of his supporters—by the notion that many visitors to his site would be eager to get involved in his campaign beyond making a cash donation. As such, his site has an activist flavor and many touch points for involvement. Such a strategy "wouldn't suit every candidate. It fits Howard Dean well," says Morra Aarons, director of Internet communications for Sen. John Kerry, D-Mass. Visitors to Kerry's site are more inclined simply to be seeking information, Aarons says.

Many of Dean's methods for raising awareness, support, and funds online will be emulated.

But the candidates are taking bits and pieces from Dean. "There are definitely tools and tricks that the Dean campaign uses that we've looked at and said, 'Oh, maybe we can use this,'" admits Mike Liddell, director of Internet strategy for Sen. Joseph Lieberman, D-Conn. Examples include posting images of Lieberman flanked by supporters (to visually illustrate the fact that he has a following) and changing the site's Weblog from a diary to an interactive feature that welcomes comments from visitors. Liddell adds, however, that "my job is not to do what Dean has done. My job is to create an online communications strategy that really mirrors our candidate."

Not everyone *can* do what Dean has done. The Internet plays to his strengths—just as TV played to the strengths of John F. Kennedy. Carol Darr, director of the Institute for Politics, Democracy & the Internet in Washington, theorizes that "charismatic, outspoken mavericks" are the ones who attract Internet followings. "Since the Internet is interactive and it requires the user to take an affirmative action, to go to a Web site, to log on to a chat room, you have to have candidates that motivate people," she says. "It's not like couch potatoes, where you just sit there and are the passive recipient of whatever commercial comes along."

It may be no surprise, then, that the three candidates with perhaps the strongest, most galvanizing personalities—Dean, Clark, and Rep. Dennis Kucinich, D-Ohio—are the ones who have gained the most grassroots Web support. For example, all three have seized on Meetup, an online service that like-minded people can use to congregate locally. (The Clark camp used Meetup to spread the word about the event at The Grand Saloon.) According to the site's figures, some 175,000 of Dean's supporters, 60,000 of Clark's, and 20,000 of Kucinich's have registered through Meetup to attend gatherings.

Dean, Clark, and Kucinich have also fared well with online fundraising, having reportedly earned nearly half of their donations through the Internet. That success allowed Dean, who reeled in about $40 million online and offline last year, to reject public financing—freeing him from spending caps in each state. It put Clark, who received about $10 million in fourth-quarter donations, in a position to make his late start. And it armed long-shot Kucinich, who raised about $1.5 million in Q4, with enough funds to continue his battle.

By contrast, Lieberman, whose campaign did not release preliminary fourth-quarter numbers, has derived only about 10 percent of his donations from the Internet, according to Liddell.

"For the first time, you have a door into the political process that isn't marked 'big money.'"—Carol Darr, Institute for Politics, Democracy & the Internet

---

And it's not just the total dollar figures involved. It's the size of the donations. It is becoming efficient for the Democrats to target small donors as they chip away at President Bush's $130 million war chest—a development that has a democratizing effect on the fundraising process. "If you're [raising money] $50 at a time, you're going to spend a lot more time and energy that's not reasonable. But on the Internet, it's not cost-prohibitive," says Brian Reich, director of the Boston outpost of Mindshare Internet Campaigns, which helps organizations advance public-affairs objectives online.

"For the first time, you have a door into the political process that isn't marked 'big money,'" Darr says. "That changes everything."

The Internet is also revolutionizing the role of Joe Citizen in the process. Three months ago, Lisa Thaler was waffling between Dean and Clark, so she visited their Web sites. The 38-year-old psychotherapist gravitated toward Clark's site, and after attending one of his Meetups, she was sold. "I haven't been involved with a presidential campaign until [now]," says the Manhattan resident, who previously made her voting decisions based on political coverage in *The New York Times*.

Thaler's story is not unique. The Web has empowered people to get involved early and often by making information and volunteering opportunities readily accessible. "It used to be this big psychological leap to go volunteer," says Darr. "Now you can just kind of dip your toe in the water. . . . You can go to a Meetup and lurk at the bar and check it out. You can proceed at your own pace."

Some campaigns have online forums or blogs to encourage an open dialogue in a non-threatening environment. This peer-to-peer communications model runs contrary to the traditional controlled, top-down, message-focused system. "The mantra has always been, 'Keep your message consistent. Keep your message consistent,'" says John Hlinko, director of Internet strategy for Clark. "That was all well and good in the past. Now it's a recipe for disaster. . . . You can choose to have a Stalinist structure that's really doctri-

McCain-Feingold Has Nothing on the Net

"Politicians love loopholes," Slate publisher Cyrus Krohn says gleefully, as he identifies a glaring one in the Bipartisan Campaign Reform Act of 2002. The rule barring independent groups from airing political ads 30 days before primaries and 60 days before general elections—meant to lessen the influence of soft money—does not apply to the Web.

The Supreme Court upheld the exemption in December, rejecting claims that the legislation—commonly known as McCain-Feingold—unfairly favored online advertising. Krohn, who also advises Microsoft's MSN on political advertising, intends to use the loophole as a sales hook, especially for MSN's ad-supported video service. McCain-Feingold "makes Internet advertising even more attractive," says Cliff Sloan, vp of business development and general counsel at Washingtonpost.Newsweek Interactive.

While they are excited about the prospect, Web publishers know they won't be welcoming a huge torrent of offline media funds. It will be more like a trickle, and much of it will go to paid search-engine placement.

Among the Democrats, Howard Dean, John Edwards, and John Kerry are the online ad leaders thus far, delivering 2.5 million, 2.4 million, and 800,000 impressions, respectively, during a seven-month period last year, according to Nielsen/NetRatings. Still, those are relatively paltry numbers. "I'm talking about .00001 percent . . . of total dollars spent in political marketing," says Krohn.

Morra Aarons, Kerry's online guru, admits his interactive ad budget is small, pointing to a recent video-ad buy on AOL worth less than $10,000. "There's never been a line item [in campaigns' media budgets] for online ads," says Karen Jagoda, president of the E-Voter Institute, a nonpartisan trade association. "It's real easy to ignore if you're a TV, direct mail, or [call-center] person."

But many Web publishers are optimistic, based on inquiries from campaigns and on the capabilities of the medium. "It allows a campaign, for example, to focus in on soccer moms in New Jersey or senior citizens in Southern Florida or young men in a particular area of California," says Sloan. "If you want [New Hampshire] two days leading up to the primary, you can get that," adds Krohn.

NYTimes.com and Washingtonpost.com can play up their access to "influentials"—readers who are well-informed, well-connected, and highly engaged in their communities and workplaces. Plus, the medium is cheap. Says Krohn: "For what you spend for one TV spot at 3 in the morning in a major market, you could have a significant share of voice on almost any Web site."

naire and that's really opposed to grassroots. Or you can say, 'Go forth. Do what you're going to do.' As long as we're running in the same direction, it's much better to give some freedom."

Before their candidate dropped out of the race, the team working for Richard Gephardt, D-Mo., made similar steps. "Having that two-way communication is what keeps people coming back to the site," says Dan Melleby, senior director of technologies at Westhill Partners, a New York–based consulting firm that was advising Gephardt's Web group. "They follow their candidate. They feel very much a part of the campaign." (Of course, relinquishing control is risky. For one thing, unsympathetic visitors—or "trolls"—can infiltrate message boards with ease. Choosing the safer path, Kerry's forum, for example, whose topics range from Iraq and foreign policy to healthcare, is overseen by a moderator.)

What's true for online marketers is true for online politicians: A Web-savvy audience is an attractive audience.

The rate of change in the use of online tools is remarkable. Despite his advocacy of the Internet, Al Gore failed to actualize its potential during his bid for the White House in 2000. "We had a fabulous Web page. But basically it just sat there," recalls Reich, Gore's former briefing director. "We had a big e-mail network, but there wasn't the real kind of segmentation that you would need to personalize e-mails and to make people feel like they were receiving something special from the campaign." Conversely, with Dean's campaign, Reich says, "I feel like I have a personal relationship with Joe Trippi," who regularly sends messages to Dean's e-mail list of roughly half a million people.

Plus, what's true for online marketers is true for online politicians: A Web-savvy audience is an attractive audience. Last October alone, nearly 2 million people visited a Democratic presidential candidate's Web site, according to Nielsen/NetRatings. While that group represents only about 1.4 percent of the 136 million total U.S. Internet users, its makeup is intriguing. It is a group that skews toward 18–34-year-old females who are better educated, visit almost two and a half times as many Web sites as the typical surfer, and spend twice as much time online. As the power of network TV continues to erode due to fragmentation and waning viewership, the Web offers a cost-efficient alternative for campaigns looking to reach this highly influential segment.

Still, online campaign expenditures remain insignificant compared with offline spending. Reich estimates that the Democratic contenders are generally putting less than 3 percent of their budgets behind the Internet—although Dean, he says, may be allocating about 10 percent.

Why the lack of investment? "The people who run campaigns largely are all in their 40s, 50s, and 60s, and they grew up in the Kennedy, Nixon, and Reagan era and those types of campaigns, where television is everything," says Reich. "So, they think television is what sways voters. You know what? Television does not sway voters. TV is not going to have the effect that it once had. But campaigns are still going to dump upwards of 60 percent of their budgets into television. Why? Because the people who run campaigns are stuck in the mold."

Yet for every Beltway traditionalist who retires, an Internet proponent like Mike Liddell, Morra Aarons or John Hlinko comes onto the scene. And once a few more Howard Deans emerge—and a few more egos are checked—the tide may turn for good. Predicts Noble: "I think the Internet will have more of an impact on politics than probably television and radio combined."

In the meantime, the unsung Web teams will keep toiling away as primary season heats up. Liddell, a University of Texas graduate who ran his own political Web site development company in Austin before being recruited by Lieberman in July, has had little time to get acclimated to life in D.C. The 25-year-old generally clocks 70- to 80-hour work weeks overseeing what he describes as a "little media empire" that requires constant updating, from issue statements and speeches to press releases, photographs, and TV ads.

Hlinko, 36, who is from D.C., looks forward to returning—hopefully victorious—to the nation's capital from Little Rock, Ark., where Clark's campaign is based. It's been a long road for Hlinko, who last April launched a letter-writing campaign via DraftWesleyClark.com to convince Clark to enter the race. The initiative, which produced more than 50,000 letters, earned Hlinko and three friends a Sunday dinner with Clark and his family at a Los Angeles hotel in early September. The following week, Clark declared his bid, and Hlinko hasn't slowed down since.

"The one thing that bums me out is that my fiancée is back in D.C. In fact, I proposed to her three days after Clark announced," says Hlinko, who has worked as an investment banker, a campaign manager, an economist, a dot-com marketing director, and a professional comedy writer. "We had a real, real nice dinner, and I took her back to the hotel where I was staying. And I had a big sign saying, 'Thank you for accepting this draft.' Then I gave her a little rock in Little Rock."

No matter the outcome, Aarons, 27, echoes what all the Democratic contenders' Web strategists say: "It's my dream job."

"There are real people out there logging on to Democratic Web sites and supporting campaigns in small amounts like they've never done before," says Reich. "People who have never voted before are probably going to go to the polls. People who have never given before are going to give and become involved in the political process. The Internet provides an incredible, never-been-seen-before opportunity for those people who feel like they have a stake in this election."

Endorsements May Help
But Not Much[9]

BY J. PATRICK COOLICAN
THE SEATTLE TIMES, FEBRUARY 6, 2004

Barbara Helen Berger is the Bainbridge Island author and illustrator of "Angels on a Pin," a picture book about a city on the head of a pin.

Berger has endorsed Dennis Kucinich to be the next president of the United States, encouraging Washington Democrats to support the Ohio congressman during tomorrow's caucuses.

Endorsements like Berger's or even from politicians like Gov. Gary Locke, who recently backed Massachusetts Sen. John Kerry usually don't move large numbers of voters from one candidate to another, political scientists and historians said.

Endorsements help to provide a sheen of legitimacy, organizational help and fund-raising help. But their influence has waned in the past two generations, and that says something about U.S. society, experts said.

"Most research indicates those endorsements don't matter at all, because people have so many sources of information," said Mark Smith, a professor of political science at the University of Washington who recently co-authored a paper on the effects of endorsements on initiative campaigns.

The reasons for the waning influence of endorsements probably have something to do with a declining faith in institutions and the leaders who run them, said a political historian. "People don't vote for an organization. They want an individual," said Douglas Brinkley, director of the Eisenhower Center for American Studies at the University of New Orleans. "You don't have Jimmy Hoffa imposing his will or delivering votes. You don't have big boss mayors delivering anymore."

He noted, however, that the right fit can give a campaign energy, citing Vietnam veteran and former senator Max Cleland, on stage with Kerry lately.

Voters are more likely to make up their own minds after consulting the mushrooming sources of information cable TV, the Web, talk radio, or talking to friends and family.

Cody Yantis and Erin Boni, undecided voters at a Tacoma rally Tuesday for former Vermont Gov. Howard Dean, said they would make up their minds based on his speech, discussions with friends whose opinion they respect, and by reading newspapers.

Jackie Stewart, who was also at the Dean rally, might pay attention to newspaper endorsements because she said she assumes perhaps naively its editors know about these things.

Ruy Teixeira, a fellow at the Center for American Progress, a think tank in Washington, D.C., said newspaper endorsements could occasionally provide a kind of "threshold credibility role; they can help put you on the map."

When, for instance, *The Des Moines Register* endorsed North Carolina Sen. John Edwards before the Iowa caucuses last month, his campaign seemed to gain momentum. He finished a surprising second behind Kerry in that contest.

On the other hand, a *Seattle Times* editorial Sunday endorsing Joe Lieberman in the Washington caucus came too late to help the Connecticut senator's campaign. He dropped out of the race two days later.

Brinkley said a candidate must choose endorsements wisely.

Edwards was running third in Oklahoma behind retired Army Gen. Wesley Clark and Kerry last week, when legendary former Oklahoma Sooners football coach Barry Switzer made automated phone calls to voters on Edwards' behalf. In a state where football is part of the civic fabric, Edwards finished a close second in the primary, nearly beating Clark.

Dean's endorsement from Al Gore, on the other hand, Brinkley said, "blew his message" as an outsider. "What outsider has Al Gore with him?" he asked.

Bibliography

Books

Aldrich, John. *Why Parties? The Origin and Transformation of Political Parties in America*. Chicago: University of Chicago Press, 1995.

Ansolabehere, Stephen, and Shanto Iyengar. *Going Negative: How Political Advertisements Shrink and Polarize the Electorate*. New York: Free Press, 1995.

Barker, Lucius J., Mack Jones, and Katherine Tate. *African Americans and the American Political System*. Upper Saddle River, N.J.: Prentice Hall, 1999.

Bibby, John F., and L. Sandy Maisel, eds. *Two Parties—Or More? The American Party System*. 2nd ed. Boulder, Colo.: Westview Press, 2002.

Cook, Rhodes. *The Presidential Nominating Process: A Place for Us?* Lanham, Md.: Rowman & Littlefield, 2003.

Davis, James W. *U.S. Presidential Primaries and the Caucus-Convention System: A Sourcebook*. Westport, Conn.: Greenwood Press, 1997.

DiClerico, Robert E., ed. *Political Parties, Campaigns, and Elections*. Upper Saddle River, N.J.: Prentice Hall, 2000.

Disch, Lisa Jane. *The Tyranny of the Two-Party System*. New York: Columbia University Press, 2002.

Donelly, David, et al. *Money and Politics*. Boston: Beacon Press, 2001.

Goldstein, Michael L. *Guide to the 2004 Presidential Election*. Washington, D.C.: CQ Press, 2003.

Gould, Lewis L. *Grand Old Party: A History of the Republicans*. New York: Random House, 2003.

Greenberg, Stanley B. *The Two Americas: Our Current Political Deadlock and How to Break It*. New York: Thomas Dunne Books, 2004.

Gregg, Gary L., ed. *Securing Democracy: Why We Have an Electoral College*. Wilmington, Del.: ISI Books, 2001.

Halstead, Ted, and Michael Lind. *The Radical Center: The Future of American Politics*. New York: Doubleday, 2001.

Handlin, Amy H. *Whatever Happened to the Year of the Woman?: Why Women Still Aren't Getting to the Top in Politics*. Denver: Arden Press, 1998.

Hillsman, Bill. *Run the Other Way: Fixing the Broken Two-Party System, One Race at a Time*. New York: Free Press, 2004.

Huffington, Arianna. *Pigs at the Trough: How Corporate Greed and Political Corruption Are Undermining America*. New York: Crown Publishers, 2003.

Judis, John B., and Ruy Teixeira. *The Emerging Democratic Majority*. New York: Scribner, 2004.

Keyssar, Alexander. *The Right to Vote: The Contested History of Democracy in the United States*. New York: Basic Books, 2000.

Maisel, L. Sandy. *The Parties Respond: Changes in American Parties and Campaigns*. 4th ed. Boulder, Colo.: Westview Press, 2002.

Mayer, William G., ed. *In Pursuit of the White House: How We Choose Our Presidential Nominees*. New York: Chatham House, 1996.

Moore, John Leo. *Elections A-Z*. 2nd ed. Washington, D.C.: CQ Press, 2003.

Palmer, Niall A. *The New Hampshire Primary and the American Electoral Process*. Westport, Conn.: Praeger, 1997.

Patterson, Thomas E. *The Vanishing Voter: Public Involvement in the Age of Uncertainty*. New York: Knopf, 2003.

Scala, Dante J. *Stormy Weather: The New Hampshire Primary and Presidential Politics*. New York: Palgrave Macmillan, 2003.

Schumaker, Paul D., and Burdett A. Loomis, eds. *Choosing a President: The Electoral College and Beyond*. New York: Chatham House Publishers, 2002.

Shade, William G., Ballard C. Campbell, and Craig R. Coenen, eds. *American Presidential Campaigns and Elections*. 3 vols. Armonk, N.Y.: Sharpe Reference, 2003.

Smith, Bradley A. *Unfree Speech: The Folly of Campaign Finance Reform*. Princeton, N.J.: Princeton University Press, 2001.

Thomas, Sue, and Clyde Wilcox, eds. *Women and Elective Office: Past, Present, and Future*. New York: Oxford University Press, 1998.

Thompson, Dennis F. *Just Elections: Creating a Fair Electoral Process in the United States*. Chicago: University of Chicago Press, 2002.

Thurber, James A., and Candice J. Nelson, eds. *Campaigns and Elections American Style*. Boulder, Colo.: Westview Press, 2004.

Toobin, Jeffrey. *Too Close to Call: The Thirty-Six-Day Battle to Decide the 2000 Election*. New York: Random House, 2002.

Wayne, Stephen J. *The Road to the White House 2004*. 7th ed. Stamford, Conn.: Wadsworth Publishers, 2003.

Witcover, Jules. *Party of the People: A History of the Democrats*. New York: Random House, 2003.

Additional Periodical Articles with Abstracts

More information about the United States election system and related topics can be found in the following articles. Readers who require a more comprehensive selection are advised to consult *Readers' Guide to Periodical Literature*, *Readers' Guide Abstracts*, *Social Sciences Abstracts*, and other H.W. Wilson publications.

Celebrity Endorsements: Decisive or Divisive? Gregory Solmon and Sandy Brown. *Adweek*, v. 45 p11 February 6, 2004.

Although political candidates can benefit from endorsements by actors, musicians, sports personalities, and other entertainers, experts say that such endorsements are sometimes more trouble than they are worth, according to Solmon and Brown. Larry Sabato, director of the University of Virginia's Center for Politics, says that celebrity endorsements can help candidates to build name identification. However, he points out that celebrities who sell things tend to lack credibility because people believe that they will do anything for money. The celebrity endorsements received by the candidates in the 2004 Democratic primaries are also discussed.

A Citizen's Guide to the Conventions. Robert B. Reich. *American Prospect*, v. 11 p56 August 14, 2000.

The writer contends that there are really three party conventions each for Republicans and for Democrats during a presidential election year. The first is the prime-time convention, televised to an ever-decreasing viewership. The second convention is for the party faithful, those who slog away at the grass-roots level, and it takes place mostly on the convention floor. The third convention, Reich asserts, belongs to the fat cats—the big-money donors to the coffers of both parties. The fat-cat conventions of both parties will be almost identical. The donors—political consultants, heads of trade associations, giant corporations, and investment banks—hedge their bets and support both parties in order to gain access to whoever gets to Washington.

New Generation, New Politics. Anna Greenberg. *The American Prospect*, v. 14 ppA3–5 October 1, 2003.

When Generation Y, born around 1980 and after, reaches voting age, it could have as big an impact on politics as the Baby Boom generation, Greenberg predicts. Even at current depressed polling rates, voters aged under 25 will constitute between 7 percent and 8 percent of the electorate in 2004. The group has members with diverse liberal and conservative political views, Greenberg says, and although the group has stopped the national slide into Republicanism, their votes remain up for grabs to the party that can find the right message and deliver it with authenticity in a medium with which young people are in tune.

Has Gerrymandering Gone too Far? Lorraine Woellert. *Business Week*, p53 December 15, 2003.

Woellert reports that within an almost evenly divided Congress, House Republicans are leaning on friendly legislatures to redraw the lines of congressional districts and establish safe GOP havens. In Pennsylvania, for example, Republicans wiped out four Democratic districts in 2002, and in 2003 newly elected Republican majorities in Texas and Colorado took the unusual step of redistricting, changing lines already confirmed by the courts. With redistricting disputes generating an ever more vicious political jungle, Woellert says, these fights are likely to land in the U.S. Supreme Court, which must decide what are the fair limits of this gerrymandering.

Inside the Dems' Shadow Party. Aaron Bernstein, Paula Dwyer, and Lorraine Woellert. *Business Week*, pp105–6 March 22, 2004.

The Democratic Party is using "soft money" and private groups to fight the Republican money machine, the authors observe. In order to circumvent the McCain-Feingold campaign-finance reform act, Democratic activists have rushed to create political committees that can lawfully collect soft money, pay for issue ads, and encourage voter turnout. Called 527s after a provision of the federal code that gives them tax-exempt status, the committees, the writers note, have been amazingly successful since they got under way last year, having already amassed nearly $100 million in soft money. More important than the money, however, the writers argue, is the very sophisticated political machine being built—a web of interlocking, like-minded organizations that could at once save and partly supersede the Democratic Party. This strategy is largely the creation of Steve Rosenthal, former political director of the AFL-CIO. He and his organization, America Coming Together, are aiming to raise $95 million to build an elaborate operation that will push Democratic voters to the polls in 17 battleground states.

Campaign Finance Reform School. Michael Scherer. *Columbia Journalism Review*, v. 41 pp54–56 September/October 2002.

Scherer reports that under new political campaign law, so-called soft money contributions that are disclosed in plain sight to the FEC will be outlawed. However, nothing, Scherer argues, will stop individuals, corporations, or labor unions from writing even bigger unregulated checks to 527s, tax-exempt political nonprofits, and other nonprofits. In the coming era of campaign finance, following the flow will be harder. The probable new routes are numerous and evolving, Scherer says, depending on future judicial rulings and a hotly disputed FEC rule-making process, but most observers say there are three broad areas to watch.

Digital Politics: Plumbing the 'Net's Power. William H. Whitney. *Columbia Journalism Review*, v. 42 p9 March/April 2004.

Whitney writes that Christopher Lydon, the erudite former host of Boston public radio's *The Connection*, has created a new Web site to chronicle the role of the Internet in general and Weblogs in particular in this year's presidential campaign: http://www.bloggingofthepresident.com. Lydon believes that this issue is not being covered well by the mainstream press, and he argues for the value of studying this new terrain and its implications. Lydon also notes that it is difficult to predict how these new forces will play out in the campaign and beyond.

Crowded Out: American Political Conventions: Part One. Philip John Davies. *Contemporary Review*, v. 276 pp12–18 January 2000.

In the first part of a two-part article, the writer examines the history of the conventions of the two major political parties in the United States. Focusing on the role of the crowd rather than on party leaders and delegates, he discusses some of these conventions and the problems encountered by the political parties in their attempts to manage the events and mediate the feelings of the crowd. In particular, he comments on the 1968 Democratic convention, in which the Vietnam War played a significant part, and the 1992 Republican convention, in which President Bush's team lost control of the proceedings as the conservative Pat Buchanan made a speech that characterized the forthcoming election as a religious struggle for the soul of America.

Crowded Out: American Political Conventions: Part Two. Philip John Davies. *Contemporary Review*, v. 276 pp74–79 February 2000.

In the second part of his two-part article, Davies focuses on the way in which media concerns, particularly those of television, dominated the 1996 Democratic and Republican National Conventions. He argues that a convention style that substitutes designer presentation for traditional debates is unlikely to overcome the skepticism with which the U.S. electorate regards its politicians. He predicts that the presidential nomination battles in 2000 will have the potential to stir up a great deal of feeling within the parties, despite the party managers' determination to reduce the impact of the political crowd.

The Electoral College and American Politics. Simon Sheppard. *Contemporary Review*, v. 278 pp344–48 June 2001.

The writer discusses the electoral college political system in America. Noting that George W. Bush won the presidential election in 2000 despite winning over half a million fewer votes than his rival, Al Gore, Sheppard argues that this is because the United States is a federal republic and not a pure democracy. Furthermore, he contends that the Electoral College, the system by which a president is chosen, is biased in favor of the Republican Party. He demonstrates that the recent reapportionment of congressional districts means every representative gained or lost in each state is also a vote in the Electoral College gained or lost, and that the new electoral map will favor the Republicans even more.

Politics to the Power of Two. Gregory L. Giroux. *CQ Weekly*, v. 61 pp2015–16+ August 9, 2003.

Democrats need to gain just two seats to win control of the Senate in the 2004 elections, Giroux observes, but with 15 months to go before Election Day, Republicans do not seem vulnerable enough for the Democrats to seize even that small an advantage. Indeed, given the obstacles they face, Giroux argues, Democrats may be just as likely to lose seats in 2004 as to win them. Details of why Illinois and Alaska are "must win" states for Democrats in 2004, of other Democratic targets, of the seats that may be difficult for Democrats to retain, and of the cash on hand held by senators as of June 30, 2003, are provided.

Swing Voters Again the Key in Starkly Divided Nation. Bob Benenson. *CQ Weekly*, v. 62 pp468–69 February 21, 2004.

Benenson reports that, just months from Election Day in November 2004, it appears that in political terms, the U.S. has picked up largely where it left off in 2000, when the nation was divided between Democrats and Republicans: Nearly all major national polls demonstrate that the public is still split down the middle on which party should control the White House and Congress. As a result, the two parties are fighting intensely over elusive swing voters on whom so many recent elections have turned, with each party grappling to add millions of independents and others who have no strong party affiliation to its base in order to win a majority. At the moment, the writer maintains, there is no political tidal wave in the offing that could either sweep the Democrats to a new era of dominance in Washington, D.C., or give Republicans an inarguable claim to being the country's majority party.

Tom DeLay's *Chef d'oeuvre*. *The Economist*, v. 369 p34 October 18, 2003.

In October 2003, a new map of congressional districts in Texas was signed into law, subject to legal review, that, according to the *Economist*, signifies a new low in politicians' abuse of electoral rules in order to gain partisan advantage. The map is the brainchild of the majority leader in the House of Representatives, Tom DeLay, even though redistricting is normally an affair for state legislatures. Redistricting—or gerrymandering—is damaging to American democracy, the *Economist* argues, because it makes seats too safe, thereby lessening the moderating influence of centrist voters, polarizing opinion, and destroying debate.

Politics as Warfare: American Politics Has Become More Partisan, and Nastier. John Parker. *The Economist*, v. 369 pp16–18 November 8, 2003.

Republican strategists think their party may be on the verge of breaking American politics' deadlock between the two main political parties in 2003, given recent electoral results, but the evidence is still against the notion that there has been a fundamental shift in politics, Parker argues. Partisanship is rife at all levels of politics and is particularly apparent in the electorate, as evidenced by a sharp decline in split-ticket voting, and the truly independent voter seems to be disappearing. Greater polarization has implications for the style of public debate, for the country's decentralized political tradition, and for President George W. Bush himself, Parker observes.

The New Soft Money. Jeffrey H. Birnbaum. *Fortune*, v. 148 pp155–56+ November 10, 2003.

Campaign-finance reform did not end big political donations but just changed the rules of the game, Birnbaum argues. McCain-Feingold, as the legislation is commonly called, sought to eliminate massive contributions from national politics, closing a loophole that allowed individuals, corporations, and labor unions to pour as much soft money as they liked into the national political parties. The act did not, however, stop funds from being sent outside the national party committee system, and party loyalists have been working to develop ways of keeping the soft-money spigot open without violating the complex law. Birnbaum discusses a number of individuals and organizations involved in garnering large political donations.

Will These People Swing? Jeremy Kahn. *Fortune*, v. 149 pp100–102+ March 22, 2004.

Kahn argues that President George W. Bush's biggest problem in the upcoming election may be the anger over the fact that he will probably finish his first term with fewer Americans working than when he took office. Jobs and the increasing federal deficit are issues that the Democrats hope to use to win swing voters and decrease Bush's core GOP support. The president's base seems to be holding nationwide, Kahn observes, but there are signs that among certain groups of traditional Republican voters, support for him is falling. This mood is particularly evident in critical states where tens of thousands of manufacturing jobs have disappeared in the past three years.

Machine Politics. Anya Sostek. *Governing*, v. 16 p33 November 2002.

Georgia secretary of state Cathy Cox, the subject of Sostek's report, has been a dedicated crusader for election reform since the November 2000 presidential elections. She has managed to push a far-reaching proposal past the legislature in time for the 2002 election. According to Sostek, her essential aim—putting touch-screen voting machines in every Georgia precinct—has produced the most important and ambitious reform anywhere in America.

The Soft-Money Crackdown. Alan Greenblatt. *Governing*, v. 17 pp34+ March 2004.

The writer examines the implications of the McCain-Feingold campaign finance reform bill for state political parties.

Rocking the Hip-Hop Vote. Kristin V. Jones. *The Nation*, v. 277 pp7–8 December 1, 2003.

Jones reports that the latest project from hip-hop tycoon Russell Simmons is a voter-registration initiative called Hip-Hop Team Vote. The venture was launched by the Hip-Hop Summit Action Network (HSAN), which Simmons, founder of Def Jam Records, set up with Benjamin Chavis, a former head of the NAACP. Attracting young hip-hop fans with such top names as Eminem, Jay-Z, Nas, and P. Diddy, HSAN has been promoting a political agenda that advocates drug-law reform, opposes education cuts, and encourages community development programs.

The Great Election Grab. Jeffrey Toobin. *The New Yorker*, v. 79 pp63–66+ December 8, 2003.

Toobin speculates on the outcome of arguments to be heard by the U.S. Supreme on December 10, 2003, in a case that could change the nature of redistricting and, with it, modern American electoral politics. Although the framers of the Constitution created the House of Representatives to be the division of government most responsive to changes in the public mood, Toobin explains, gerrymandered districts mean that most of the 435 members of Congress never face seriously contested general elections. The Court has long held that legislators may not discriminate on the basis of race in redistricting, Toobin notes, but the issue that the Court faces in this case is whether, or to what extent, they may consider politics in defining congressional boundaries.

Black Box Voting Blues. Steven Levy. *Newsweek*, v. 142 p69 November 3, 2003.

Election officials are embracing sleek, touch-screen terminals known as direct recording electronic voting systems (DRE), Levy notes. Unfortunately, according to Rep. Rush Holt of New Jersey, the machines have a fatal disadvantage in that they are unverifiable. When a voter votes, he has no way of being sure that the vote is recorded, he says. Furthermore, the best minds in the computer-security world maintain that the voting terminals cannot be trusted. To solve the problem, Levy reports, technologists and allies are advocating a scheme called verifiable voting. This supplements electronic voting systems with a printout that affirms the voter's choices and goes immediately into a secure lockbox to be tallied if there is need for a recount.

Ballot Breakdown. Wendy M. Grossman. *Scientific American*, v. 290 pp16+ February 2004.

Grossman describes the continuing efforts in the U.S. to address concerns about computerized voting. The Help America Voting Act was enacted in October 2002 to modernize voting systems across the U.S. The intention was to computerize the current system where voters use punch cards. Grossman reports, however, that the Institute of Electrical and Electronics Engineers, which was given the task of modernization, has been unable to come up with a solution that satisfies everyone. The main concerns expressed have to do with security and voter verifiability. Some progress, nevertheless, has been made, writes Grossman, and the solutions appear to be paper-based. They include a 2-part paper ballot that allows the voter to see how the ballot was cast but ensures that no third party sees the result, and ballot boxes that are equipped with a glass screen and printer that enables the voter to recheck his choice.

Bring on the Cash! Matthew Cooper and Karen Tumulty. *Time*, v. 163 pp18–21 February 23, 2004.

While President George W. Bush and Democratic front-runner John Kerry trade blows in public, the real battle, Cooper and Tumulty explain, is taking place behind the scenes as both sides try to find new ways to raise funds. During the past 12 months, Democrats have been trying to find exemptions in the McCain-Feingold campaign-finance-reform law they themselves supported. One route they are hoping will be fruitful, according to the writers, is a network of new organizations known as 527s, which are allowed to raise unlimited funds for advertising and voter-registration drives, provided they do not coordinate with the candidate. For their part, the Republicans can count on well-heeled big donors and a well-oiled fund-raising machine that moves with relentless efficiency.

The Vexations of Voting Machines. Viveca Vovak. *Time*, v. 163 pp42–44 May 3, 2004.

Technological problems are causing many people to question the reliability of e-voting systems, Vovak observes. The technology was supposed to guarantee an end to the difficulties that plagued the 2000 presidential election, the result of which depended on subjective calls regarding hanging and pregnant chads. After that messy conclusion, election officials in 34 states, from Florida to California, bought so many e-voting machines that approximately 50 million people, or over one-third of registered voters, are expected to use them in November. Primary-season problems and a general concern about sending votes down an electronic black hole have led to a backlash, however, Vovak reports. Numerous voter activists, computer scientists, and elected officials have joined a growing movement to either make the systems more accountable or abandon e-voting entirely.

The Latin Swing. Reed Karaim. *U.S. News & World Report*, v. 135 pp12–15 September 8, 2003.

Both Democrats and Republicans say they are about to capitalize on America's Hispanic voters, Karaim reports. With Latino culture associated with a traditionally Democratic economic liberalism and a traditionally Republican social conservatism, Hispanics appear to offer opportunity to both parties. The results of a CBS–*New York Times* poll are quoted concerning the number of undecided Hispanic voters, and the writer discusses Democratic and Republican efforts to woo them.

An American Krakatoa? Roger Simon. *U.S. News & World Report*, v. 136 p35 May 24, 2004.

Simon argues that despite expectations of an extremely close 2004 presidential election, the most likely outcome is a landslide victory for John Kerry. The second most likely scenario, he says, is a huge triumph for President George W. Bush.

Electoral College. Joel K. Goldstein. *Update on Law-Related Education*, v. 20 pp34–6, 1996.

Goldstein takes an all-encompassing look at the electoral college, describing its history and how it has functioned over the centuries. He also presents both sides of the argument over whether the system should be discontinued.

Hack the Vote. Michael Shnayerson. *Vanity Fair*, pp158+ April 2004.

According to published reports, Shnayerson writes, touch-screen voting machines made by four major companies have immature technology and weak security. By November 2, 2004, these companies, three of which have links to wealthy Republicans, will be tallying votes in the presidential election in almost every state of the union. For over 10 years, entrepreneurs have been developing touch-screen DREs—direct recording electronic voting systems—that could replace various paper-ballot systems and cumbersome lever machines. As Shnayerson explains, the election disaster of 2000 made them sought-after commodities overnight, leading to the enactment of the Help America Vote Act on October 29, 2002, with its vision of an electronic voting machine in every polling place. The writer discusses the work of Seattle freelance writer Bev Harris, who has campaigned to highlight weaknesses in DRE technology and discrepancies in the results of elections in which DREs were used.

Whither the Sprawl People? *The Wilson Quarterly*, v. 27 p85 Winter 2003.

An overview of two articles from *Blueprint* magazine summarizes the positions of John B. Judis and Ray Teixeira, as well as David Brooks. Judis and Teixeira argue that, despite the Republican successes in November 2002, the Democrats are poised to benefit from the diffusion of the post-industrial economy, in which "the production of ideas and services" looms large. The bluish (Democratic) new politics, their analysis claims, is being molded by the growth of "ideopolises"— metropolitan areas in which the suburbs have become more urbanized. Brooks, on the other hand, asserts that the people who live and work in the sprawl areas have no "regular contact with urban life. They live in a nascent culture of their own that is neither red (Republican) nor blue.

A Vote for the Electoral College. Gary Glenn. *Wilson Quarterly*, v. 27 pp89–90 Spring 2003.

The writer argues that the Electoral College system is more democratic than any practical alternative.

Index